FATHERHOOD *Is* LEADERSHIP

Praise for *Fatherhood Is Leadership: Your Playbook for Success, Self-Leadership, and a Richer Life*

Devon Bandison has scored big with this entertaining and inspiring book that every leader and every father will want to read right away!

~ **Steve Chandler,** author of *Crazy Good: A Book of CHOICES*

Fatherhood Is Leadership is a great parenting resource written by my friend, Devon Bandison. Devon's the real deal. He's been there and done that. Let him guide you through the process of creating the dynamic you desire with your children, whilst at the same time giving you a swift kick up the ass. He'll remind you that you are the greatest role model for your children, that you are just what they need. Lead not just by showing up in the lives of your children but by showing up in the world as well. Buy it now. Invest in yourself and your children. You won't regret it!

~ **Stella Reid,** author and star of the television show *Nanny 911*

Thank you, Devon Bandison, for giving all fathers – and the mothers and children who love and depend on them – a great gift with this wonderful book. It's filled with heart-felt and hard-won wisdom that is as practical as it is profound. Bandison shows by example how he's striving to live the life of a passionate and reflective learner. His fearless search for knowledge, mainly about who he is, has enabled him to be a dedicated and generous teacher, converting the lessons of his experience into tools any father can use to become the leader he wants to be.

~ **Stew Friedman,** author of *Total Leadership* and *Leading the Life You Want*

You know that good feeling you get when you learn something that you'll use for the rest of your life? Read *Fatherhood Is Leadership* and you'll be on the fast track to influence and success. Fathers, mentors and community leaders alike will benefit from applying Devon's tactics to achieve success.

~ **Jason W. Womack,** MEd, MA, author of *Your Best Just Got Better*

We often meet dads who feel hopeless and helpless as they face challenges at work and at home. Devon Bandison's underlying theme throughout *Fatherhood Is Leadership* is that overcoming each of these challenges starts and ends with us. Bandison uses his own life story to share the tools that he has developed in himself to become the man and father he envisioned. His life experiences and proactive approach will benefit dads of all stripes.

~ **Matt Schneider & Lance Somerfeld,** Co-Founders, City Dads Group

This book is a game changer!!! Devon Bandison takes us on a journey through life and fatherhood, sharing his challenges and triumphs as a young man and developing into a fatherhood leader today. Throughout the book there are lessons for all of us and activities we can use to grow as people and fathers. This book is filled with solutions. Fatherhood is indeed a leadership position and to be a leader, one must be prepared. This book does just that, and will propel you to new heights. After reading it, you will be transformed; you will never see yourself or fatherhood in the same light again.

~ **Derek Phillips,** Founder & Executive Director of Real Dads Network

We've come a long way in our society to where we undeniably recognize the value and impact fathers have in the lives of our children, our families and even our country. Fatherhood for all its value is still an everyday work in progress. Using great storytelling and his own unique experiences, Devon Bandison captures our attention with each chapter. He takes us on a journey filled with life lessons and shares the pain & joys of fatherhood. Along the way he learns that his destiny—and our own—is to be the best father he can be, and this vision is defined by his sense of self, purpose, leadership & success. Never before has there been a playbook for fathers that connects us directly to our inner leader and offers us a guide to success and a better life for ourselves and our children—until now.

~ **Thabiti Boone,** Former White House Fatherhood Initiative Representative

Devon Bandison masterfully weaves powerful trials, lessons, and gifts from his own journey as a father and leader with practical and immediately applicable exercises to help you become a truly present and connected parent. More than that though, he shares the essence of what real leadership looks like—both in the lives of your children and in your everyday life. You now hold in your hands everything you need to be the man you know you are capable of being.

~ **Jason "JG" Goldberg,** MBA, International Speaker + EDU-tainer + Author, King of Playful Sales, Success, and Self-Leadership

Devon Bandison's groundbreaking book on fatherhood shines a clear light on the value of being present in the unfolding story of your child's life. Devon shows how perfection is not the key but that honesty, integrity and humility are the way forward to being the father who offers leadership through love and quiet, mindful, intentional examples. Thank you, Devon, for this important book on what fatherhood looks like. I am sure it will change many lives.

~ **Jane Evans,** International & TED Talks Childhood Anxiety and Trauma Speaker, Author, Coach and Consultant

Fatherhood Is Leadership is an incredibly refreshing read covering a very multifaceted topic: fatherhood! Author Devon Bandison has delivered a vividly descriptive parenting resource that is both practical and thought-provoking. *Fatherhood Is Leadership* effectively displays the complex intersections between fatherhood and positive male role modeling, fatherhood and healthy masculinity, and fatherhood and male socialization. Devon remarkably intertwines both his personal and professional experiences in such a way that individuals across all socio-economic spheres will be able to relate. A must read!

~ **Larry D. Edwards,** LMSW, Edwards Mentoring & Social Services, Founder / Director

This is so much more than a book. It's more like a literary work of art that doubles as an annihilator of the old-school paradigm. When they talk about, say, the "works of Alan Watts," well, this is one of the "works of Bandison." It's simultaneously hilarious, hip, tear-jerking, inspirational and life-altering. And it could only be crafted by someone who has clearly committed years of his life to deep healing and personal and spiritual growth. I'm not a father. And yet I had absolutely no difficulty finding personal significance in the lessons that Devon so masterfully conveys through his remarkable litany of entertaining stories. This is a must read, especially for fathers, but certainly not only fathers—for everyone.

~ **Philly Boy, Chris Dorris,** Author and Mental Toughness Coach

This is the one book every father should read! When we drop our expectations, our perspectives change, which changes our world and the way we see it. This book can help anyone stop the struggle and start living an extraordinary life!

~ **Trevor Mulligan,** stay-at-home dad and City Dads Group Co-Founder/Organizer

FATHERHOOD *Is* LEADERSHIP

Your Playbook for Success,
Self-Leadership, and a Richer Life

DEVON BANDISON

MAURICE BASSETT
books for athletes of the mind

Fatherhood Is Leadership: Your Playbook for Success, Self-Leadership, and a Richer Life

Maurice Bassett
P.O. Box 839
Anna Maria, FL 34216

Contact the publisher:
MauriceBassett@gmail.com
www.MauriceBassett.com

Contact the author:
www.devonbandison.com

Edited by Chris Nelson
Cover design by Carrie Brito
Front cover photo by Albie Mitchell
Back cover photo by Mindy Veissid

ISBN: 978-1-60025-097-2

Library of Congress Control Number: 2017910420

First Edition

DEDICATION

This book is dedicated to Kaila, Justice, and Omari. Three beautiful souls who have profoundly influenced my life more than anyone. Thank you for teaching me way more than I could ever teach you about love and life. Because of you, I am a better father, son, friend, brother and man. I love you with all my heart.

TABLE OF CONTENTS

INTRODUCTION

To whom much is given, much is required.

As fathers, we are given the greatest gift of all in our children. When my first child, my daughter Kaila, was born, I experienced what every new father feels the first time he holds his child in his arms. I cried tears of joy. My heart opened, and I felt love in a way I never had before. From that moment I felt the need to protect and love my daughter. Life made sense in a whole new way.

Fathers today tend to be more involved and better parents than at any other time in history. We're attending school meetings, helping with homework, walking our kids to school, changing diapers and sharing in other co-parenting responsibilities. We're spending time talking things over with our children and sharing our own choices, struggles and joys, often as a way to help them with their own. The impact is monumental. Children with active fathers have better grades, experience less depression, have an easier time adjusting to life changes, and make better choices.

My own work with fathers takes it a step deeper. The leadership qualities that create impact in children's lives are the same ones that impact the world. The fathers I work with understand this. In our work together they discover for themselves that *fatherhood is leadership.*

As someone whose life-work has been dedicated to leadership development and fatherhood, the synergy is clear—and the payoff is extraordinary.

In this book, I'm going to ask you to question what both fatherhood and leadership mean to you. We'll dig deep, and I'll ask you to reexamine everything you've been told about what it means to be a man, a father and a leader. In the process you'll acquire a new lens and a sharper focus. You'll see yourself, your family and the world in a whole new way.

The fathers I've been honored to work with over the years have embarked on this same exploration and experienced miraculous breakthroughs in their lives, relationships and work. They have created a living legacy—something they can be proud of *now*, while they're still here to enjoy their families, their work, their lives.

Today the greatest leaders understand that the only true way to lead is by example. Actions speak louder than words. Leadership is not about titles—it's about one life influencing another.

The exact same thing is true in modern-day fatherhood. Fatherhood isn't about your title. It's not about "do as I say, not as I do." It's about how your actions and the examples you set impact the lives of others. As fathers, the way we show up to lead profoundly influences our children, our spouse, our family, our community and, ultimately, the world.

In other words, we're up to something BIG here.

Fatherhood Is Leadership is the playbook for a movement that sets out to shift the old-school, authoritarian paradigm towards a new, intentional, heart-centered, service-focused and conscious form of self-leadership. It is, I believe, the next step in the evolution of the modern father. Our goal is nothing less than the transformation of our lives from the inside out. From this space we can increase our influence, improve our intimacy and maximize our positive impact in our relationships with our loved ones and the world.

When I sat down to write this book I realized we didn't need another "how-to" parenting book. I wanted instead to open a dialogue in which men could see not only that we aren't alone, but also that we already have everything inside ourselves to create the love, relationships, success and financial freedom we desire.

After years dedicated to working in the trenches developing fatherhood programs, navigating through and learning from my own challenges, and now living a life beyond anything I could have imagined, I understand the meaning of the saying, "To whom much is given, much is required." Or to put it in a more modern, but equally true way:

With great power comes great responsibility.
Peter Parker (Spider Man)

We have a responsibility to our children, and part of meeting that responsibility means seeing ourselves in a new light and celebrating the amazing gifts that fathers bring to the world.

I don't want to just crack open the door on a father's impact on the world—I want to bust it wide open.

I have seen firsthand, in my life and in the lives of the powerful men I work with, that a renewed focus on fatherhood and leadership can change the world. In fact, if we open ourselves to it, fatherhood can be the gateway to freedom.

Yes, believe me: it's that powerful.

But it's an inside job, and it starts and ends with you.

Throughout this book I'll share stories—my own and others'—about the challenges of modern-day fatherhood, about the wins, the losses, and the ever-present opportunities we have to create a living legacy for ourselves and our world. After most chapters there's a section called "The Legacy Zone." This is the place where we distill the essence of the chapter into practical tools. These are the same tools I've used with some of the highest-performing leaders in the world. They'll work for you, too, if you give yourself the second greatest gift of all (after your kids!): the gift of your own attention.

Trust me: it's worth it. *You're* worth it. And if you practice the leadership skills, mindset and habits we'll explore together, the impact on your family, finances, and community will be greater than anything you've ever imagined.

I've used these tools to coach professional athletes who thought life was over after retirement, only to reinvent themselves in the world while improving their relationships with their children and families.

I've used them to help a father whose authoritarian parenting style caused him to lose connection with his children. By working on himself he created a loving new environment for his loved ones. The transformation was so powerful that it encouraged his son to enter drug and alcohol rehab, and he now works with his father to run the family-owned, multi-million-dollar company.

I've used what I share in this book to help a stay-at-home dad who felt like he was losing his passion for life. He loved being a videographer but didn't know if he had time to follow his dream. After working with me for six months he launched his own side business in New Mexico, becoming the go-to guy for real estate agents—using his videography skills to help sell houses. And he did this while remaining true to his commitments as a stay-at-home dad.

I've used these ideas with fatherhood groups around the country and seen them engage entire communities.

My hope is that you'll use this book to spark a fire within yourself, a fire that gives you permission to reinvent yourself and become the best father, the best leader—the best *man*—you can be.

On Children

Kahlil Gibran

Your children are not your children.

They are the sons and daughters of Life's longing for itself.

They come through you but not from you,

And though they are with you, yet they belong not to you.

You may give them your love but not your thoughts.

For they have their own thoughts.

You may house their bodies but not their souls,

For their souls dwell in the house of tomorrow,

which you cannot visit, not even in your dreams.

You may strive to be like them, but seek not to make them like you.

For life goes not backward nor tarries with yesterday.

You are the bows from which your children as living arrows are sent forth.

The archer sees the mark upon the path of the infinite,

and He bends you with His might that His arrows may go swift and far.

Let your bending in the archer's hand be for gladness;

For even as He loves the arrow that flies,

so He loves also the bow that is stable.

1

FRIDAY NIGHT PIZZA NIGHT

The miracle of love comes to you in the presence of the uninterpreted moment. If you are mentally somewhere else, you miss real life.

~ Byron Katie

It's Friday, and in anticipation I leave my office at 4:00 p.m.

I never schedule afternoon meetings on Fridays. My personal commitment is to leave no later than 4:00 to catch the 4:09 train to New Jersey, but as any New Yorker knows, subway times are affected by stalls, sick passengers, police activity, and so on. A three-hour journey can easily become four hours or more. So today I've left early.

My priority is picking up my son, Omari, from elementary school, and I don't let anything get in the way of that.

As I get off the train and walk to Omari's school, I reflect on my journey. I'm filled with gratitude for all we've been through. I've created a life centered around the things I value most. I'm grateful to show my son that his father loves him and will be there for him despite any obstacles along the way. I'm grateful for the inner work I've done and for the strength it's helped me develop.

Some of the fathers I coach haven't been able to experience this level of empowerment yet because circumstances, mindset and choices make their reality difficult. It's not always easy for fathers—for anyone—to create an intentional life. We have all kinds of demands at home, on the job and in relationships. As providers and protectors we've got financial and safety concerns, and we also think about the impact we want to have on our families and the world.

I've learned from personal experience and through the fathers I coach that creating the kind of life I now have is possible. It takes effort, but the payoff is extraordinary.

I can usually tell how engaged Omari is by whether he runs and jumps into my arms—sending chills of joy down my spine and a smile to my face—or whether he puts up a fuss with a tear or two at the thought of ending his basketball game early. I've learned by now from my two older children not to take this personally. It's not about me or even the love my son has for me. It's about him in the present moment. Meeting my son where he is, validating his feelings and letting him know that there's enough fun to go around usually squashes any reluctance to make our way to Penn Station together.

Today, however, is a good day.

Omari shouts, "Daddy!" and runs down the hallway into my arms. This is joy! After a long moment I put him down, and while he gets his coat and backpack I speak with his teacher about how he's doing in school.

Then we're on our way.

By the time we arrive at Penn Station our stomachs are growling. My son puts out his arms with a look that clearly says, "Pick me up!" So I do. I carry him up all forty-three steps (yes, I've counted!) from the New Jersey transit platform to the Long

Island Rail Road area in Penn Station. I have my bag over one shoulder and his backpack on my back. He's heavy, I'm tired and the people in front of us never seem to move fast enough up the stairs. But when he puckers up and lays a big kiss on my cheek I forget all that. This moment amidst all the noise and chaos is priceless. His kiss is one of appreciation for my being his hero.

We make our way to our famous pizza joint in the heart of Penn Station. The place is buzzing with out-of-towners, commuters and regulars like us. The smell of melted cheese and fresh pizza crust fills the air. The guys behind the counter recognize us and prepare our usual order: four cheese slices, two of them cut in half. My son takes great pride in being able to open the fridge's display door to grab himself a soda and me a bottle of seltzer water.

We find seats near the bathroom and the feast begins. In between bites, we talk about his day and whatever else is on his mind. Sometimes it's Ninja Turtles, sometimes school, sometimes basketball, but it always ends with one question: "Will my brother be there when we get home?" If Omari's older brother Justice isn't at basketball practice or out doing whatever teenagers do, then the answer is "yes," and this brings a big, bright smile to his face.

Before we leave we make a stop in the bathroom. There are few things more stressful than being on an hour-long train ride with a five-year-old who can't hold it anymore.

It's the dead of winter and freezing cold in NYC—the weather app says seventeen degrees, but it feels much colder. Thankfully the pizza shop in Penn Station is connected to the subway station underground so we don't have to wander outside yet.

Although the subway is packed, there's often an unspoken connection with the strangers who see a father and his young son together. Immediately a man offers up his seat to Omari. Without hesitation (well, maybe a little NYC hesitation) a woman offers her seat to me so I can sit next to my son. I thank them both. Their smiles show they're happy to have done a good deed.

Omari lays his head on my lap, his eyes looking heavy. I ask, "Are you tired?"

Without hesitation he offers an unconvincing yet emphatic, "No!"

Less than a minute later he's passed out on my lap. I laugh inside at the fact that I can only recall one time when Omari actually admitted he was tired. My belief is that he looks at time spent sleeping as missing out on something. He can't miss a second of this great big, amazing world in front of him. If he admits to feeling tired, it's like he's admitting defeat. Sleep isn't an option, until it is.

I glance down at my son, asleep under the brim of his blue and white tassle hat, his Air Jordan sneakers tucked beneath his legs. He's bundled in a blue bomber jacket and has his backpack on his lap. His warmth and innocence are palpable. It's a BIG city in a BIG world for this five-year-old traveling the iron horse with his dad in the underground tunnels of New York City.

I feel complete.

There's no place I'd rather be than right here, right now.

***

I treasure these moments with Omari. Words like connection, unconditional love, gratitude, freedom, abundance and peace come to mind to describe my feelings in moments like these, but really there's so much more going on inside me. Only a father can understand the magical feeling that occurs in these brief moments of silence after a night like the one I've had with Omari.

Our journey has been nothing short of challenging. When Omari was three-and-a-half years old, his mother and I went through a difficult divorce. Any breakup is difficult, but when children are involved it's even more painful. Soon after our split, Omari moved in with his mother. At first my son only spent every other weekend with me. But that wasn't enough. We needed more. I felt we were missing out on one of the most important connections of all, the one that develops between a father and his child. I knew I needed to do whatever I could to change our situation.

Throughout the breakup I had been on an emotional rollercoaster. I felt helpless, sad, angry, hurt, guilty, remorseful, ashamed—you name it. But in spite of this, Omari's innocence and light shone through to my heart, inspiring me to shine even brighter. I realized my son is an amazing being. He sees me as if I can do no wrong. He looks to me for love, guidance, wisdom, protection, comfort and laughter. His light inspires me to step into my higher self, to commit more than ever to showing up as a full-time father despite a part-time living arrangement—and regardless of financial concerns, adversity or difficulties in my relationship with his mother.

My mission is simple: to show up as the best father I can be.

This is my calling. If I fail at this, nothing else matters. Now I know that when I stand up and am the best version of myself, I create a space for this adorable and special being to nurture the seeds of his own highest self: LOVE.

My journey to this point started with me doing inner work on myself. I decided to give myself the gift of my own attention. This included hours of reading, practicing, experimenting, and talking to other men about fatherhood, relationships and life. I began to see the importance of self-care and daily routines that include some sort of mindfulness and meditation.

From my conversations with other men I've found that most still get stuck in talking about their feelings and struggles. Most of them have difficulty asking for help. Three themes emerge time and again:

1. **Performance:** Fathers worry about having what it takes to be a "good father," however they define that.

2. **Security:** Fathers are concerned about providing protection and financial security for their families.

3. **Mortality:** Fathers are aware of their own limited time and are concerned about their legacy. They want to provide their children with the emotional and practical skills necessary to navigate life.

The time I dedicated to myself ultimately transformed how I showed up as a man and as a father. This work was key to me becoming the man I needed to be and addressing the three concerns above—and much more. It allowed me to be more present, clear-minded, and emotionally balanced, as well as less anxious.

I'm not talking about being perfect. I fall short of my ideals often enough. But one of the keys to success and fulfillment isn't seeking perfection but developing a practice that works for you, one that helps you regularly show up at the top of your game.

This was true whether the situation involved a divorce, tough news about my two teenagers, finding out my son was being bullied or just me, sitting at home feeling less than complete at times. My commitment to self-care and self-love allowed me to be at my best more often than not. What's more, knowing that this state of mind was always available to me was key to my sense of freedom—or "FREE-DOME" (aka free mind)—which meant less confusion, negative self-talk and doubt.

The coaching clients I started sharing these insights with, and who also began similar practices in their own lives, started reporting the same shifts. They were less reactive and much more present.

This was a modern-day miracle for all of us.

The ability to not overreact to every curveball life throws our way allows us to be the owners of our lives, our well-being, happiness, fulfillment and our relationships with our children.

We are not victims of circumstances.

Can you see what a powerful shift living from this awareness could bring to your life?

With my newfound dedication, I began to emerge as the father I knew my son deserved. I was present, playful, patient, kind, authentic, supportive, strong and loving. As a result of committing to my own transformation, time with my son shifted from every other weekend to every weekend, as schedules allowed. This required commuting two-and-a-half hours each way from Queens to New Jersey via public transportation to pick Omari up from school on Friday afternoons, and then waking up at 5:00 a.m. to do it all in reverse on Monday mornings to get him to school on time.

No problem.

Our "Friday Night Pizza Night" kicked off weekends of connection and healing together. I still look forward to them each and every week. The journey has all been worth it just to experience moments like these.

The inner work I've done on myself to transform my mindset and my choices has allowed me to become the man, the father, the friend, the son, the business owner, and the leader I have always wanted to be. I feel such freedom living without the guilt, the shame or the remorse. I wake up excited about the days ahead.

What's more, I can clearly see the benefits my transformation has had on my three children—Omari, his teenage brother, Justice, and my daughter, Kaila, currently nineteen and in college.

Our journey hasn't always been easy, but it has been well worth it. While divorce is never ideal, I've created a reality many fathers struggle to find. Omari can be with me for up to twelve out of thirty days a month, one full month in the summer, and on holidays. That's a far cry from what it could've been.

I continue to be a work in progress, but the feeling inside of me is one I know other fathers may also sometimes get glimpses of. I'm showing up as best and as powerfully as I can. I've not become a victim of circumstances. I've taken ownership over my relationships and the time I spend with my son. Regardless of distance, divorce or anything else, I've made choices to create my life. In this intentionally created life there is no more fear, shame, guilt or regret.

Too many times I've seen and heard stories about fathers who allowed circumstances to determine their relationships with their children. I'm here to tell you that there is another way to live.

I started this journey by asking myself two questions: "What is missing from my life and how am I keeping it out?"

My answers led to choices that would ultimately create my

future reality. They shifted me from helpless to hopeful, sad to happy, heavy to light. Love is my highest self, and from that place, miracles happen.

The answers led, for example, to Friday Night Pizza Night, a ritual that created a space for us as father and son to heal, bond and create a new reality. In this sense, PIZZA is the healthiest food my son and I have ever eaten.

***

Fathers, I get it.

You're not just a father. You might be an employee, business owner, husband, baseball coach, and more. You're a hard worker. You wear a hundred hats and struggle to make sense of them all. You care about your family. Maybe you don't have a vision of what success as a father and in life would look like for you. Maybe you didn't have an active father when you needed one most. Maybe you're a father who has all the outside trappings of what you think success looks like (car, house, picket fence, 2.5 children), but you feel unfulfilled, uninspired and lack passion.

I get it. I've been there, and I've coached other men who have been there too. As a father to three wonderful children and a successful business owner and success coach, I know from experience the challenges we face as men and fathers out in the world. There aren't many resources available for those focused on creating a fulfilling life while raising children.

I'm here to change that.

I'm here to provide you a safe space to change your life. A space where together we can explore influence, intimacy and impact so that we can dig deep and learn what you want and how to bring it about. This book is written for you.

Here's the good news on what's possible:

- We already have what it takes to be great! Great in business, great as parents and great in terms of the positive impact we can have on society.

- We can achieve career success and financial freedom without losing out on priceless, intimate moments with our families.

- We can serve our children in a way that is so incredibly profound it will help us lay a foundation for them to be even better and more successful than we are.

- We can rebuild and redefine relationships in powerful ways and communicate effectively and creatively with ourselves, our spouses and our children.

- We can achieve our goals, follow our passions and live as our most authentic selves without apology.

Sound good?

My research and expertise focus on two areas: fatherhood and high-performance leadership. I've worked with some of the most successful athletes, business owners, CEOs, high achievers, and everyday fathers who want more out of life. In this book I share my personal experiences of transformation as well as disciplines and tools from my coaching practice. What's most exciting to me is that you don't need to be a CEO or have a stacked bank account to benefit from what I'm sharing.

This book is for ALL FATHERS. PERIOD!

I'm so grateful for all the experiences in my life. I'll share many of them with you, raw and uncut, in the hopes of reaching as many fathers as I can. My story includes all aspects of the human experience from a father's perspective—love, pain, happiness, fear, joy, fulfillment, abundance, achievement, service, perseverance, commitment, friendships, heartbreak, ownership, victimhood, fatherhood, co-parenting, children, spirituality and completeness.

My aim in this book is to be an instrument of service and a source of inspiration. I'm committed to changing the fatherhood story—permanently. This book comes from my heart with the intention of reaching other hearts—any hearts, whether loving, broken, in pain or full of joy. I want to provide you the tools that will help you become a better father, a better man, and a better leader—and create miracles in your life.

Remember: It all starts and ends with YOU. If you want to be a better:

- Father—it starts and ends with you.

- Husband—it starts and ends with you.

- Partner—it starts and ends with you.

- Friend—it starts and ends with you.

- Leader—it starts and ends with you.

- Server—it starts and ends with you.

- Boss—it starts and ends with you.

- Employee—it starts and ends with you.

- Human Being—it starts and ends with you.

My hope is that you'll take what you need from this book and leave the rest. And that after you apply what you've learned and see amazing shifts and transformations in your life, you'll pay it forward. Share the gifts you receive by serving others. Take this information and turn it into transformation by applying it in your daily life. Serve your children, spouse, family, friends and community.

Your world will change, and in turn you will change the world.

2

BED-STUY, DO OR DIE

Leadership isn't about your title, position or flow chart.
It's about one life influencing another.

~ John Maxwell

I started my first job after graduating college in 1997, one month after my daughter was born. I was hired as a Social Worker Assistant at a non-profit organization working with "at-risk" youth—children and young adults ages five to eighteen who struggled with mental health, behavioral issues and emotional problems. My job was to provide supportive counseling and mentorship to them.

This work grew to be so inspiring that I eventually referred to the young people I worked with as "at-hope" youth. I wanted to be a vision of hope for young people, many of whom suffered in silence like I had done as a teenager. As a first-time father I had a great sense of purpose to provide for my family, and I was excited to change the world.

After training for only two weeks, which included reading through charts, shadowing other workers during in-home visits and attending weekly supervision meetings with my manager, I was thrust into the work. My first solo case was a young man I'll call

"Sean."[1] Sean had been hospitalized seven times in the previous year for emotional and behavioral issues and had jumped from foster home to foster home. Now he was being reunited with his mother. My job was to first assess his safety and then create a behavioral intervention plan based on his needs.

Sean and his mother lived in the Bedford Stuyvesant section of Brooklyn, also known as Bed-Stuy (sounds like "bed-stye"). Brooklyn is the largest of the five boroughs that make up New York City. It's rich with cultural history and community, so it's no surprise that the residents carry a lot of pride. Brooklyn is also the birth place of many famous people, including Michael Jordan, Shirley Chisholm, Mike Tyson, Spike Lee, Neil Diamond, Jimmy Fallon, Al Capone, Barry Manilow, Lenny Kravitz, Larry King, Jimmy King, Clive Davis, Omar Epps and Ol' Dirty Bastard—just to name a few.

In 1997 Bed-Stuy had a uniqueness and grit that Spike Lee captured in his movie *Do the Right Thing*. Back in those days it was a rough neighborhood. People living in Bed-Stuy were known for the tough and boastful mantra, "Bed-Stuy Do or Die." But behind all of the grit and seriousness, there was a glimmer of hope that things could get better. There was strength in the community, a feeling that even though they might not have it all together, together they could have it all. Bed-Stuy was a rose growing through the cracks in the concrete.

Bed-Stuy had its challenges. If you weren't from New York, you probably wouldn't venture there without being accompanied by someone familiar with the place. But I loved it. I loved the

---

[1] Names and identifying details in this and other client stories in this book have been changed for privacy reasons.

people. I loved the vibe. I loved the carefree feeling I got walking through the neighborhood on a summer day. Kids played freely in the water bursting from open fire hydrants, a woman sold icees on the corner block, music blasted from boom boxes, and the courts were packed with men and women playing handball and basketball. Of course there were cyphers, too—the most intense freestyle rap battles you could imagine.

But the neighborhood vibe could shift in the blink of an eye. Kids went from playing in the fire hydrants to taking cover from guns firing bullets that didn't discriminate. Music gave way to police sirens. Icees were replaced by drugs. That carefree feeling could vanish in an instant.

It was vital to be aware of your surroundings in Bed-Stuy, because any sign of weakness or indication that you weren't from around there put you at risk. I made sure to walk with confidence, but even though I typically felt at ease, I maintained an edge and awareness that only residents of NYC during that time could know.

Sean had just moved into his mother's two-bedroom apartment in Bed-Stuy the month before I was assigned his case. Sean had known his father for the first seven years of his life before losing touch when his parents went through a difficult breakup. Subsequently his father had been deported to Jamaica and Sean and his mother lost contact with him. Now Sean had no father figure in his life.

In preparing to visit Sean I read through his chart. It included transcripts from sessions with therapists, social workers and probation officers. The notes indicated he had a history of anger management issues that manifested in verbal and physical altercations and a desire to harm himself. This last impulse had resulted in his first inpatient hospitalization, which was followed by several more for various other serious behavioral outbursts. He had spent the last year split between inpatient hospitalizations and short stays at Spofford Juvenile Detention Center in the Bronx. Spofford (in operation from 1957-2011) was notorious for extremely poor living conditions and child abuse. It was not an easy place to visit, let alone stay in. You could be excused for thinking a place like Spofford could only exist in a third-world country. Many boys went in there and came home forever changed, stripped of their dignity, exposed to violence and forced to mature far more quickly than they would have been on the outside. Of course, being in Spofford also gave some kids a sense of "street cred," where they felt a distorted pride in having survived being locked up there.

I arrived at Sean's home for my first visit on a hot afternoon in the middle of summer. The block was alive with sound, but there was a silence inside of me. I stopped just short of the steps and looked up at the building. Sean and his mother lived directly across from the housing projects in a two-family brownstone that looked like the Cosby's home on *The Cosby Show*. For the first time since receiving the assignment and reading Sean's chart, I paused to think about what I was about to do. For a moment, I felt overwhelmed with despair and anxiety, and I lost my sense of focus. I felt ill-prepared for what I knew was a tremendous responsibility. The negative chatter in my head told me that I couldn't help this family. Who was I to think I had the skill-set to make things better and help change this young man's life? What experience did I have? How could I make a difference? I remembered having a similar feeling only a month earlier at the birth of my daughter. As an excited first-time father I didn't think I was ready to be responsible for her life.

But as I stood at the bottom of the steps to Sean's home, I used the silence to regain my confidence and reconnect myself to my purpose. I didn't know it then, but allowing myself these brief moments of silence throughout my life would give me the opportunity to connect to the clarity, courage and focus I would need to put one foot in front of the other. Beneath it all, what was really motivating me was that I didn't want to let this young man down the way I had been let down growing up. I wanted him to know he was not alone and that there was hope for a better way of life.

There were two doorbells next to the doorframe. I took one more breath and let it all go, then walked up the steps and pushed the bottom bell for the first floor.

I heard some commotion inside the home, then a middle-aged woman dressed in a freshly pressed, white nurse's uniform opened the door. She conjured up a smile as she greeted me. Sean's mother, "Ms. C.," was originally from Jamaica. I knew from reviewing Sean's case that she worked long hours to provide the basic necessities for herself and her son. Soon Ms. C. would leave for a twelve-hour evening shift at Woodhull Hospital, not too far from their house.

The home appeared well-kept and organized. The front room was neatly decorated with knick-knacks and other cherished items. I was familiar with the phenomenon of what many families back then called their "show room." The couch against the wall wore a plastic cover, guaranteeing it would never get dirty. Some of my family members had similar rooms with similar plastic-covered couches. As kids we were forbidden to enter. I never understood this. What's the sense of having a couch if you can't sit on it?

Ms. C. offered me something to drink. I politely declined, telling her I'd just finished a bottle of water, mindful not to come across as disrespectful. She called for Sean to come to the living room, then sat in a chair. I sat on a couch, one without plastic on it. Moments later Sean entered the room and took a seat without saying a word, barely meeting my gaze. He was a tall and lanky fourteen-year-old young man resembling some of the best basketball players I knew. His arms were folded, his eyes cast down to the floor. Everything about him said he was unimpressed by my presence.

Strangely enough, my quiet confidence began to grow. All of a sudden my worry and concern dissipated. I knew beyond the shadow of a doubt that I could help this young man. His resistance and prior difficulties—and my own lack of training—no longer mattered. I had more than enough confidence, willingness and strength in myself to make a difference in his life.

I didn't know how I'd do it, but I knew I could.

Sean, like me, had been exposed to things that forced him to grow up prematurely and lose some of his innocence along the way. It was obvious from his demeanor that he had experienced betrayal and trauma. He was not going to open up and trust a complete stranger. But for some reason this no longer bothered me.

Ms. C. sat in the chair with a look of concern. She seemed to have little confidence that I, a twenty-three-year-old kid, could make a positive impact on Sean when everyone else who had tried—hospital employees, social workers, child protective service workers and juvenile detention officers—had failed.

Despite this I made a decision. I turned to Ms. C. and politely asked her if it would be alright if I had some alone time with her son. I suggested that she and I talk after I spoke with Sean.

She looked surprised. I'm sure that until now everyone else had followed the requirements of the standard assessment visit: ask the parent a barrage of questions, assess the problems and launch into what the program does and how it can help. I was going off script. In truth I didn't yet know how I could help Sean. I just knew I could, and that using the standard approach wouldn't add to what I'd already learned from his chart. I was more interested in what Sean had to say. I cared less about what had happened in the past and more about who was sitting in front of me right then: a fourteen-year-old young man who was hurting.

Sean met my eyes with a glance. I wasn't sure whether he was nervous or confused. He was probably thinking something like, *Why would this guy want to talk to me first?* or *Here we go again, another social worker trying to figure out what's wrong with me.*

Ms. C. got up from her chair and left the room.

I asked Sean how he was doing. The first ten minutes of our conversation consisted of responses like "Good," "No," "Yes," and "I guess." Then I asked Sean if he knew why I was there, and he offered, "I guess because of what's been going on."

BAM! That was the opening I'd been waiting for, a chance to engage without pushing him away. I said, "Well, I don't really know what's going on, Sean. All I know is what other people say, and I'm really not concerned with that. I just want to hear from you, because I think you know you more than anyone else. Do you agree?"

Sean hesitated, then with a slight grin responded, "Yeah, but everyone else thinks they know me, but they don't."

I now felt at ease because I knew I had a chance to show up for this young man and connect at a level that no one else had yet. I said, "How about this? I feel you, and I understand how frustrating that could be, everyone thinking they know you better than you do. Would you be willing to give me the real story about how you think things are going with you?"

There was a long, awkward silence, but I continued to make eye contact with Sean as he contemplated what I had just asked of him. Finally he nodded "yes" and began to share his thoughts.

The foundation of our relationship and work together began in that moment. Sean shared some insights around his relationship with his mother and what he thought about school. I gave him some background on me about my days of playing college basketball and talked about some of the tournaments I played. He seemed impressed, and I felt like we connected. I steered clear of anything regarding his past during my first visit. I didn't want him to feel judged. Our conversation was light, and we even shared a laugh or two. Our connection cracked the hard exterior he'd had when he first entered the living room that day.

Two days later I returned to officially begin my work with Sean for the next two months. Our scheduled visits were intensive, conducted every Monday, Wednesday and Friday in his home after school. We worked on developing his coping, anger management and socialization skills. To my surprise some of what I had learned in training was useful, but it was awkward to teach the first time. Sean shared with me that he had recently wanted to "wild out" at school, as he would say, but he used a counting technique I had taught him to calm himself down.

I began to see some major shifts. A young man was

developing right in front of my eyes.

Approximately two weeks into our work together Sean had an altercation at school. I believe it could've escalated into something far worse than it did. When I spoke with Ms. C. about the incident, her voice was tight yet respectful.

"This isn't working," she said. "He isn't making a change."

I felt crushed. My biggest fears—that I couldn't help this young man—were coming true. I kept silent for a minute and thought about the shifts I had seen in Sean. Then I regrouped, took a breath and validated Ms. C.'s frustration. After that I shared the progress I had witnessed. I talked about Sean's willingness to be open and honest and to consistently show up for our appointments. I also asked Ms. C. to take a longer view of what was possible.

Ultimately I convinced her that Sean was open to change and was, in fact, making changes. When I urged her to give the intervention a chance, she agreed.

Within a month of starting our work together, Sean smiled more often. He even cracked some jokes. He opened up about everything from sports to girls to music. He even started talking about the absence of his father and about how he questioned his father's love for him.

For my own part, I was excited to wake up and go to work each day. I felt like each time I arrived something even more miraculous happened. This wasn't about either of us being perfect and always saying or doing the right thing. This was about the space we created for commitment, trust, honesty, openness and a willingness to step outside our comfort zones. This allowed for the unfolding of something that hadn't seemed possible only a few weeks before.

The impossible had become possible. This is my definition of a miracle.

Sean's grades improved, and so did his relationship with his mother. They were talking, eating dinner together and even agreed to a movie night at least once a month. In conversation one afternoon, Ms. C. told me that she had noticed how much better Sean responded when she validated his hard work and effort. Until recently she had been expecting perfection instead of progress.

I felt a quiet satisfaction as she spoke, but I was caught off guard by what she said next. "Devon, thank you so much for all you are doing. Because of you, I have my son back."

Words can't adequately describe my feeling at that moment. I was overwhelmed with joy, compassion and love. I felt accomplishment and hope, tempered with some uncertainty as to what the possibilities were for Sean after our time together ended.

I said, "Ms. C., thank you. It was you and Sean who put in the work and allowed me into your home to help create this change."

This was true. I was just the conduit through which this beautiful relationship between mother and son could begin to flourish again.

Midway through our work together, I asked Sean, "What vision do you have for your life? What are your goals, your dreams and aspirations?"

Sean looked at me with a little bit of bewilderment and said, "Mr. B., nobody's ever asked me that. Nobody ever really cared what I wanted for my life." He shared his desire to be the first in his family to get his master's degree and have a career in music.

Upon hearing this, I reached out to my friend Jason, who ran a music program in New York City. We chatted and made plans for

Sean and I to visit the following week. When we arrived, we walked into an environment brimming with energy, creativity and excitement. Young people were singing their hearts out onstage, with equally impressive young musicians accompanying them on saxophone, trumpet and violin. Jason took us on a tour. The music program had everything Sean could have wished for and more. His eyes lit up when he saw a studio equipped with a microphone and EQ board. He declared with excitement that he wanted to produce music.

He started the program the following Saturday.

I told Sean, "My only agreement with you is that you agree to show up. If you don't feel comfortable in participating, fine, but still show up." He not only showed up but also excelled in the program.

In two months of working with Sean we were able to stabilize his behaviors and connect him with continued support. We had reached our goals. He was doing well in school, communicating with his mother, and excelling in the music program. My work was done.

***

Five years later, I'm in downtown Brooklyn, New York, on my way to Junior's Restaurant & Cheesecake to meet a friend. As I walk down Fulton Street I hear somebody yelling my name.

"Mr. B.! Mr. B.!"

I turn around and am thrilled to see Sean. I give him some dap (a handshake) and a hug. Sean is now a bright, nineteen-year-old man. He looks good: dressed nicely and beaming with pride.

"How you doing?" I ask.

We take a seat on the benches near Fulton Street and catch up.

Sean tells me he's just completed his first year of college and still has the goal of graduating with a master's degree. He also shares that he's just signed as a producer to a MAJOR record label.

I have goosebumps. These are the exact goals he had identified five years earlier during our work together. My heart opens up. I feel overjoyed hearing about his success and say, "Sean, you had a pretty tough start to your life. What was the turning point?"

He pauses then says, "Mr. B., when you came to my house, it was the first time somebody gave me hope when I felt hopeless. You gave me a voice when I felt I had no voice. When you came to my house, Mr. B., you gave me choices when I thought there were no choices." He ends by saying, "You were like the father I never had."

As I listen to Sean, I feel love in my heart, as well as a sense of connection and pride for the role I played in his success.

As we part ways, I reflect on my work with Sean, my job and my family. A lot has transpired over the past five years. My daughter is now five years old, I have a one-year-old son, and I'm in the midst of developing programs for fathers, children and families at one of the biggest non-profit organizations in the country.

I ask myself, "What did I really offer this young man?"

Obviously I wasn't his biological father, but he identified me as someone who filled that void.

In reflecting on this meeting with Sean I've come to realize that it all boiled down to leadership: I offered Sean leadership. Not by way of my title, position or authority. No, I demonstrated leadership through influence.

Leadership through influence means being aware of the fact that your actions and the examples you set impact the lives of those around you. Like leadership, fatherhood isn't about your title, position or authority. Fatherhood is about how your actions and examples impact lives.

My afternoon with Sean was a transformative experience in my life. It shifted how I viewed my ability to really make an impact on the world. I was a changed man from that day on. I became someone who looked at even the most basic interactions as opportunities to serve and make a difference.

I could've treated my interactions with Sean as "just a job." Instead I made a choice to fully commit to him by leading with my influence and staying present. I realized that you don't always need the newest invention or breakthrough to change the world. You can do it one relationship at a time, one conversation at a time and one kind act at a time.

This choice I made to lead with influence impacted how I parented as well. I choose to allow my children the space to grow into who they are meant to be, not who I want them to be. Gone are the days of "do as I say, not as I do." That mentality is outdated and antiquated, and it flat-out doesn't work (at least not for me). Leadership has just as much to do with my actions and choices as with what I say. My children always pay more attention to what I do than to what I say, as did Sean.

Children really want to be heard. They often have more insight and foresight than we give them credit for. The precious time we spend with our children offers amazing opportunities to create the space for hope, choices and possibilities in their lives and our own.

In Sean's case, I made a commitment to show up, stay the course and be open. So when I asked him to do the same, he had a model of what that looked like.

Seeing Sean pursuing his dreams years later inspired me. I was touched that he gave me credit for having had such an impact on his life, but in truth his impact on me was far greater.

He had become my teacher.

Fathers, remember: you are your children's first mentors, gurus and coaches. So own it! When you can step more fully into your leadership and recognize the power of influence, you'll see that it's much more fulfilling to live in a place where your words match your actions not only as a father, but also as a man, a son and a spouse.

Fatherhood is leadership, and leadership is influence.

Now, let's look at how you can translate your own experiences to develop your own leadership vision and style as a father through the following exercises.

THE LEGACY ZONE

Let's get to work! Complete the following exercises to help assess and develop your own leadership fathering style.

Note that as we begin "The Legacy Zone" exercises, I am going to ask that you use a journal to complete them. Journaling is a great way to process and awaken the creative part of your brain. The process of journaling both positive and negative feelings has been shown to decrease stress and have a positive impact on your health. So pick up a journal or a spare notebook and let's get in the zone of creating your legacy.

Remember, too, to experiment with these exercises. They're not meant to bog you down. They're here to help you explore issues you may have only touched on before, and to offer some tools that will make life easier and more fulfilling. Play with them, experiment, and use what works for you.

PROGRESS NOT PERFECTION

1. Can you identify where in your life you are looking for perfection rather than progress as a father (either from yourself or from your child)?

2. What can you acknowledge and celebrate TODAY about your parenting that shows progress?

3. What can you acknowledge and celebrate TODAY in your child that shows progress?

To make acknowledgments most impactful, make them part of your daily routine. Verbalize and celebrate your wins and the wins of your child in your daily conversations.

VISION AND MENTORSHIP

1. Write down your own personal vision of success. What does success look like in your life?

2. Ask yourself what support you need to achieve your vision of success AND be fulfilled.

3. Sit down with your child and ask them about what most excites them. What are their dreams?

INFLUENCE

1. Ask yourself how can you best support the dreams of your child.

2. Where in your life can you show through your actions that you are a leader?

3

THE PROMISE

Forgiveness is unlocking the door to set someone free
AND
Realizing you were the prisoner.

~ Max Lucado

I was born with basketball in my blood. Both of my parents were coaches and referees. They say the first gift I received out of the womb was a basketball left in the crib for the day I arrived home from the hospital.

I started playing competitive basketball when I was six years old. My dad was my idol and my coach, and our life together was connected by basketball. By the time I was nine, I started playing for the top Amateur Athletic Union (AAU) teams in New York City, which included Riverside Church, Madison Square Boys Club and Aim High. I wasn't the best player in the city, but I played my best and felt invincible by the time I entered high school on Long Island, where I lived with my mom. I continued to improve my game and received a scholarship to Belmont Abbey, a small college in North Carolina that was a part of the NAIA (National Association of Intercollegiate Athletics).

Back in the day my father ran City Wide, the most famous and successful basketball league in New York City. As the director, he oversaw every part of the summer and winter tournaments, and he was treated like a celebrity. City Wide was the place to play if you wanted to play the best—and you had to be the best to play. I met lifelong friends, mentors and people who became family there.

I loved basketball, but I loved being around my father even more. I felt special being known as "Butch and Dottie's son." In summer I couldn't wait to wake up at the crack of dawn, get dressed and be at the park by 6:30 a.m. Once there we'd set up the courts in time for the first game at 8:00. Games were scheduled all day from 8:00 a.m. to 6:00 p.m. around the city. I was in basketball heaven. Picture a sold-out gym or park with standing room only. The places were so full they had to turn people away at the door. By the time I was seven I had learned how to keep the scorebook and sat at the scorer's table during some of NYC's most historic games. There I was, just a kid with the best seats in the house, right next to my father as he ran the whole thing.

I got to know all the great players. Every time a basketball legend wanted to check into the game he had to come through me. I met playground legends like Mark Jackson, Kenny Anderson, Chris Mullin, Kenny Smith, Pearl Washington and Lloyd Daniels, just to name a few. I had access to all of them, the greatest players in the world. Anyone in NYC who claimed to have any skills had to have played in City Wide. The best of the best would team up from every New York borough to ball each summer and winter.

What a life! Imagine being a kid with topnotch players knowing your name or giving you nicknames like "Lil Boogie," "Lil Man" and "Shorty." I felt so big in this big world. Words can't describe the confidence it brought to me as a boy. City Wide was magical. And it felt like one big family. No matter where you lived or how far you travelled, this was a place where people all came together as one over basketball. Young or old, everyone was a part of it. That's one of the things that made it so special.

As for the game itself, basketball coaches back then considered players student athletes. Players had to bring report cards to practice each week in order to play. The coaches really cared about our education and well-being. They wanted us to become good people. They taught the game of life through the game of basketball.

And my father was the greatest teacher of them all. Our train rides, car rides and walks would be filled with stories about great players. I soon realized that the stories were less about basketball and more about life. This, I see now, was my father's tool, his way of imparting values to me the best way he knew how.

I still remember my dad telling me stories about Joe Hammond, a player who had more promise than anyone. Legend has it that he scored seventy points in a game in Rucker Park on Dr. J. His career never materialized because drugs took him out. He also told me the story about Connie Hawkins, whose NBA career started later than it should have because of an alleged point-shaving scandal that derailed him. His crime? He allegedly accepted $200 because he was broke and had no money to eat.

Through these stories my father was teaching me about making better choices and staying clear of drugs and bad influences. I didn't realize then how much those stories contributed to many of the values and principles I hold today.

My father didn't just run City Wide. He was also a coach and referee. He actually met my mother, another well-known coach and referee from a different part of Queens, through Catholic

Youth Organization (CYO) basketball. I felt like I was born into basketball royalty and had the greatest parents in the world.

***

My mother is white and my father is black, and being a biracial couple in the 1970s was tough. They faced a lot of challenges, including friends who cut them off and disrespected their relationship, but they made sure that I never felt different as a biracial kid growing up in NYC. The first six years of my life (what little I can recall of them) were fine. I don't even remember my parents arguing. I never knew that my dad got involved in doing drugs and later became addicted. My mother always kept me protected from that. So when my parents separated, it caught me totally off guard. Drug addiction will do that to families. It destroys the fabric of loving relationships without warning. It's a lethal punch, stronger than any uppercut Mike Tyson could deliver.

I do remember the day my mom packed me and our belongings into the car and left my father. I felt confused, alone and scared. They eventually divorced, and my view of the world and what it meant to be a man started to change.

I missed my parents being together. After the separation my father played only a sporadic part in my life. On the weekends I was scheduled to be with him I usually stayed with my grandmother, Oma, in Queens. My dad made the occasional cameo appearance. Nonetheless, I looked forward to spending weekends and summers with my dad's side of the family and was always happy to see him when I got the chance.

My grandmother played a very influential role in my upbringing. She was the rock of the family and made me feel special with her loving words and amazing cooking. She was a wise woman from Jamaica who immigrated to America in her teens to find a better life with my grandfather. She had met him when he served in the Dutch Army and was stationed in Jamaica. They married soon after meeting one another and eventually moved to NYC.

From what I could piece together through conversations I heard over the years, my father and his siblings had a tumultuous upbringing. There were stories of my grandfather verbally and physically abusing Oma. Really, these were more like whispers that we'd catch bits of but could never fully understand. Back in those days, being a child meant you were supposed to be seen, not heard. So we never questioned what actually went down with Oma. All I knew was that she was a strong woman who held everyone together with her love and commitment to family. This resulted in my aunts and uncles having to take sides, but everyone sided with Oma and against my grandfather. This split strained the relationship between my grandfather and his five children. Eventually Oma pulled away to create a peaceful life in a different Jamaica: Jamaica, Queens.

She often sat in the window and was the go-to person on the block for everyone to stop by and have a chat. She cooked the best steak and potatoes you'd ever taste. Her signature dish was chicken on a stick with an amazing peanut butter dip that no one—and I mean no one—could ever duplicate. In fact, a few years after her passing my mother and favorite aunt tried to make the dish for the family. It wasn't good, and we had to kindly ask them never to do it again out of respect for the legacy of Oma.

Those were fun times I spent with my dad's side of the family, and I'll always cherish them. I was devastated the day I picked up the phone at age fifteen and heard my father tell me that Oma had passed away. It was a huge blow to the entire family. Every one of my aunts and uncles took it hard, but my dad seemed to take it the hardest. He began to regress and not talk as much. He became very isolated, which was a huge contrast from the gregarious and always positive man I had grown to know. Eventually he disappeared.

Over the next couple of years he slipped deeper and deeper into drug addiction. When I was seventeen I'd drive from Long Island to Queens to check on him. One summer day I drove to his house, but when I approached the driveway I had a funny feeling in my gut. Something seemed off. As I walked down the driveway to the back door I saw people I didn't recognize walking in and out. When I opened the door I was greeted by a cloud of smoke and people who looked like zombies. The basement had been turned into a full-out crack den.

I looked for my father, but he wasn't there, so I left. It was all so surreal. I couldn't believe this was happening in my life. It was one thing to know my father had an addiction. It was another altogether to be in the middle of a crack house that was supposed to be his home.

I began blaming myself for my father's struggles. I asked myself, "Why did he choose drugs over me?" as if I had had the power to control any of that. As I walked to my car I saw him in the driveway. He was skinny and his eyes were blank and spaced out. I felt hurt and then angry and then, in an instant, vindictive. I lashed out with words, trying to hurt, guilt and shame him. I said some things that shouldn't be repeated in this book. I was grasping for instant gratification, for anything that could get rid of the pain I was feeling. But it didn't work, I still felt really sad when I got into my car and drove away.

Over the next few years I never gave up on my dad. I visited him when I could. But I also didn't forgive him for many years, even after he eventually got clean.

When we look at our lives, what's often missing is empathy for our parents and their experience, what they've gone through and struggled with. Many people tell stories about how their parents are the reason they don't trust others, are hard on themselves, became addicts, have bad relationships, struggle at work and whatever else you can fill in the blank with.

For years I blamed my father for my own struggles with alcohol abuse and my failed relationships with the mothers of my children. I held on to the story that my parents' divorce and my father's absence and addiction left me to fend for myself with no real male role model. That seeing my dad as a shell of himself in my teen years made me struggle with who I was and what it meant to be a man.

But I was fooling myself, like many of us do. In truth, we are where we are in our lives because of our *choices*, not because of some predetermined fate set in motion by the shortcomings of our parents. Our parents are just easy to use as scapegoats when we don't take responsibility for our own behavior and choices.

Today I work with both men and women who, like me, have held on to victim stories that continue to plague their present. As Byron Katie says, "Fear is always the result of an unquestioned past imagined as a future." The work on myself began when I started to question my stories as a way to find forgiveness and peace from within. I realized that my father did the best he could with the set of tools he'd had at the time. His upbringing and perception about life and who he thought he was affected his ability to cope. And although I'm not a psychologist, I understand the effects of trauma on people's behaviors and choices.

Whatever your story is, and we all have one, you can let it go. Stories can affect anyone, no matter your race, creed, color, religion, where you live or how much money you have. It's called being human. We've all created stories that, when left unexamined, have the ability to block our mental and spiritual growth.

Don't get me wrong, it took commitment to some deep internal work on my part for me to discover and experience freedom from my story. I had struggled to forgive for years. I had held tightly to this story that my father and his absence were to blame for my own struggles. Somewhere along the line I had bought into this notion that other people were responsible for my lot in life, and I became a victim of my circumstances—not the author of my own life. I told myself a story about how I was abandoned by my father and had it so hard. This story kept me in a mental prison that affected my relationships, my level of success and my ability to be the best man I could be.

But then I realized it was only a story. A story created in my head that ate up much of my time, energy and mental bandwidth. The fact is that, yes, I'm biracial. Yes, my parents divorced. Yes, my father did drugs. Those are the facts. But what story had I created out of them?

I told myself that my father didn't love me. I told myself I was unworthy of acceptance because they called me "Oreo," so I had it harder than others. I told myself it was my fault that my parents got divorced. But that was a complete fabrication scripted in the most dangerous place in the world: the space between my two ears. When I discovered I had the power to wake up to reality I was able to let it go. In letting go of past resentments I was able to be free in the present to create a future full of unlimited possibilities. In reality, I loved my childhood. I have so many great memories! And if I'm honest, I wouldn't change it for the world.

I know it can be hard to consider letting go of some of your BIG stories. I understand. So let me help you get a feel for the freedom that's possible.

Take a glass of water and hold it with your arm straight out in front of you. Ask yourself, "How much does this glass of water weigh?"

Keep holding onto the glass! Think about it. How much does it weigh? Give up?

The answer is that it doesn't really matter! It all depends on how long you hold onto it. If you hold the glass of water for a minute, there isn't really an issue. If you hold onto it for an hour, your arm will likely hurt and cramp up. If you hold onto it for a day, we're talking some serious pain and trouble. In each of the scenarios, the weight of the glass of water has not changed. But the longer you hold onto it, the heavier it becomes.

This same principle is true for the stories you've been holding onto in your own life. The stories you've created about your past hurts have been affecting your ability to be the best, most present and loving parent you can be right here, right now. These stories are your glasses of water. The longer you hold onto them, the heavier they become. Eventually they wear you down.

So put down the glass of water, and put down your stories. Let them go.

Once I was able to separate the events (facts) from the story I had created with them, I realized I didn't have to do anything to my story. I didn't have to change it, move it, process it, relive it, or go to therapy to work through it. All I had to do was LET IT GO. What was possible after that?

Miracles.

Let me tell you about one of them. In early November 2016, my father, my son Justice (who was in tenth grade at the time) and I spent an evening together in midtown Manhattan. We watched a movie based on the life of Kenny Anderson, a basketball player whom my dad and I both knew from back in the day with City Wide in Queens. Kenny was a child basketball prodigy, the greatest NYC high-school basketball player to hit the playground since the great Kareem Abdul-Jabbar (back then known as Lew Alcindor). Kenny was just a couple of years older than me and was by far the greatest high-school player I've ever seen. He had a crazy handle with the ball and a smooth left-handed jump shot that always seemed to hit the bottom of the net. People came from across the city and country just to see him play in a summer league City Wide game. He once gave his friends watches that *Sports Illustrated* sent him when he was featured as the best ninth grade basketball player in the country. My friends and I looked at Kenny like he was a basketball god. He later went on to play professional basketball for several teams, including the New Jersey Nets and Boston Celtics.

To get to the screening we took an Uber car into town from Queens. We were each looking sharp and were excited for the night to begin. But I also knew that seeing a documentary about Kenny would bring up a lot of memories—some exhilarating and some sad—for both me and my father. As we drove to the screening I thought about the days I'd spent looking over my shoulder during warmup on the layup line, hoping my father would come to coach my game. But he never did. I also remembered how amazing I'd felt when he introduced me to the top college coaches at a game in Queens.

We made our way to a restaurant down the block from the theatre on 23rd Street in Manhattan, where we'd later catch the documentary. There we sat down for dinner and began reminiscing about the "good old days." By the big smile that soon crept over his face, I could see that my father was in his element. He'd been clean for over seventeen years now and was an amazing grandfather to all my children, especially Omari. It brought joy to my heart seeing the relationships he was able to have with them.

Our food arrived and we dug in. It was great: the "old school" was meeting the "new school." Justice was now part of a tradition that had started many years back. His generation has a saying that "Ball is Life." For me, life was explained through the lessons of basketball, and to watch it come full circle with my father and son at the same table was as rewarding as a game-winning shot.

About fifteen minutes into our meal, a guy walked up to our table and said to my dad, "Hey, you may not remember me, but you were my coach when I was a kid, and I wanted to thank you. You were the best coach I ever played for."

My father's famous smile told us just how touched he was. He gave the guy the universal acknowledgement of a head nod. It was obvious he didn't really remember the man, who was one of thousands of kids he'd coached. But it didn't matter. It was a moment in time when all was well. There was no guilt, shame or regret about past times.

My son was impressed. As I glanced at the man's table, I realized he was sitting with another childhood ball player who had recently offered to help Justice transfer into his school to play basketball. Justice was in the process of coming to live with me full-time, so we found the best academic school in my area that also had a great basketball team. It just so happened that the coach was also a City Wide alumnus, which made everything possible.

That dinner offered an amazing moment that brought all three of us closer together. I didn't view it through memories of times when my father wouldn't show up. I was present, free and in a spirit of acceptance, all because I had done work on releasing my story.

FORGIVENESS

I have learned that forgiveness is vital for my growth and transformation. Forgiveness frees me from my bondage to the past. For many years I resented my father for being absent and "choosing drugs over me." I had originally used this resentment as fuel for being the best father I could be. In fact, many of the fathers I work with make what I call "The Promise." Fathers who didn't grow up with the best father figure in their lives and who want to do something different for their own kids often make a promise that sounds something like: "When I become a father, I'm going to be a better one than my father."

I made this promise as a teenager, but when Justice was young I realized that it was incomplete. It was only when I took The Promise to another level that I became a more complete father, a more complete man and a more complete human being. I forgave myself for creating the story about my father that left me disempowered for so many years. I saw that forgiveness is less about the other person than it is about you. Forgiveness is about freeing yourself from your past. Forgiveness is allowing for a more positive and loving future.

I worked on this chapter the day after our night out, and as I was writing I received a text from my father. I was so touched I had to stop writing because I got too emotional reading it.

Just want to take a moment to thank you for yesterday. I am so encouraged by you and your relationship with Justice. You are doing a great job as a dad. Your love for him shines. You're my Hero. Much love.

Can I just take a moment to let all fathers know how powerful that text is? Over the years my father had been hard-pressed to give me credit for being a father myself. I was searching for this kind of validation long before I forgave my father and released the story I'd created about him. The beautiful thing is that with all the work I'd done on myself, when I let go of my story I no longer needed validation from him or anyone else. I truly found freedom. I know who I choose to be as a man and father, and it's not based on a need for anyone else's validation.

I'm free in the here and now.

THE LEGACY ZONE

Activity #1: "Freedom from Your Story"

Take some time to reflect on the stories you've been holding on to. These stories might be days, months or even years old. Think about a specific incident and write down in a journal what happened and how it made you feel. Think about how much of an impact that story has had on your relationships or on some other aspect of your life.

Next, create a new possibility of how you'd like the relationship to be now. Once you've done this, read on below.

The following exercise will be based on the specific memory you identified and wrote about above.

1. In your journal or on a blank sheet of paper write down the situation. (Example: "My father was addicted to drugs and was an absent parent.")

2. Draw a large circle around those words and label the top of the circle "The Event."

3. Right next to that circle write out what happened as a result of that event. (Example: "My father didn't love me. I wasn't good enough. His drugs were more important than me. It's his fault that I'm struggling in my life.")

4. Draw a large circle around what happened and label the top of the circle "The Story."

5. Look at the two circles side by side. Notice that there is "what happened" and then there is "the story" you created as a result.

6. Now write out what you see as true. (Example: "The truth is that my father did have a problem, but the story that told me I wasn't good enough and that he was the cause of my struggles was totally made up in my head.")

ACTIVITY #2: "FORGIVENESS AND FREEDOM"

1. Sit quietly and think of a problematic relationship you have not yet resolved, one for which you continue to hold feelings of resentment, shame, anger, or something else. Explore your thoughts and feelings and find where you've been holding on to material that doesn't serve you.

2. When you've processed these feelings, call that person and/or write a letter telling them how you felt in the past, how you feel now, and the part YOU played in the relationship being the way it is. Discuss the impact that your belief has had on the relationship.*

3. Create a new possibility for that relationship, and stand in that new possibility.

EXAMPLE:

"Dad, I've been inauthentic. I've held this resentment about you for years and created a story that you had abandoned me. The impact of that belief is that I've been walking around angry with you, which hasn't allowed for us to become as close as we could.

Today, I stand in the possibility of compassion and love. I want to create a relationship that is rooted in understanding and compassion so that we can have a meaningful relationship moving forward."

After you have spoken, be quiet and listen to what they say.

* You might need to modify this method if the other person is, for example, no longer alive. In such cases, you can still write a letter communicating your feelings, and this in turn will empower you to create a new relationship for yourself, one that lets go of the old stories that have been holding you back. The breakthrough here comes when you realize that your story is NOT TRUE. It's only your interpretation of what actually happened. Think about how long you've been making decisions based on a story you created days, months or years ago. Without that story you now can create anything (any relationship) you want. You are no longer a prisoner to that story.

4

BEST SEATS IN THE HOUSE

The present moment is the only moment available to us,
and it's the door to all moments.

~ Thich Nhat Hanh

"Dad, this was the best day of my life."

Justice and I were riding home on the Long Island Rail Road
when he said this to me. We were on our way back to Queens from
the Barclays Center after the 2012 NBA Draft.

As his father, it was an amazing feeling to be part of
something so significant in the eyes of a teenager. Justice is an
amazing young man. He has all the qualities of someone who will
make a great leader someday. He's smart, funny, charismatic and
gifted in sports and in the classroom. He lights up a room with his
quick wit and sense of humor.

He is also the most amazing big brother I've ever seen:
kind-hearted, loving and always willing to wrestle or hang with his
little brother, Omari. Omari idolizes him, which is a pretty cool
dynamic to watch. At thirteen he's at an age where he's going back
and forth on whether or not he wants to truly commit to playing
basketball throughout high school, and that's okay. I want him to
make his own decisions about what he'd like to pursue, without

any pressure from me. He and I spend time talking about everything from sports to politics to sex to drugs and hip-hop. Our relationship is special in that way, and I appreciate him greatly. I remember driving him to school when he was five years old, pumping "The Good Life" by Kanye West through the speakers of my Audi. This song reminded us then that life is always good, and that's still true.

My cell phone had rung around 2:00 p.m. earlier that day. My father was calling to tell me that he'd promised to take his grandson to the NBA draft but didn't realize that the tickets cost money.

I hung up the phone, shaking my head, and with a chuckle inside I said to myself, *You didn't realize they cost money? Really, man? C'mon!* I could almost feel those old bugaboo thoughts creeping up on me, trying to penetrate the newfound peace I have in my life. All those past resentments about how I felt my father had let me down.

In the past I would've taken the opportunity to guilt my father over his past transgressions, but I'm a different person today—a different man, a different son and a different father. I've evolved not by acting like I know all the answers but instead by going back and questioning my own answers. I see now that I've grown *because* of my relationship with my father, not in spite of it.

So I put my phone away, packed up my things, headed out of work and jumped on the 5 train from Manhattan towards the Barclays Center in Brooklyn to show up and take over. I'd had a long day serving corporate clients, teaching them how to communicate effectively and work as a team. And while I love my work, I was looking forward to seeing my father and son.

As I rode the train, I remembered my own first draft experience. I had been thirteen years old, too. Back in 1987, a guy from the neighborhood named Mark Jackson was in the NBA draft. He was one of the players dominating the City Wide games. My dad got us tickets and I was beyond excited for my very first draft experience. In fact, being drafted to the NBA was my own dream at that age. I spent ten to twelve hours each day every summer playing ball in the park, hoping that one day I'd be on the Felt Forum stage having my name called. It was amazing to see someone from my neighborhood making it to "The League."

At the NBA draft I felt BIG, like I was a part of something special: a lineage, a legacy, a path laid out before I'd even been born. The energy in the Felt Forum (connected to Madison Square Garden) was palpable, and all of NYC was excited to hear their hometown hero, Mark Jackson, get drafted by our beloved Knicks. We chanted, "We want Mark!" followed by "Don't fuck up!" When his name was called, everyone burst into a deafening roar and joy filled the entire arena. Grown men hugged each other, and I turned to my dad with a giant smile on my face and gave him a high-five.

That moment was everything. It was perfect. There were no worries, no anger, just love and joy.

Now it may sound weird that a sporting event could bring out these kinds of emotions, but not if you loved the game like I did. Even to this day, when I see a miraculous feat by an athlete, it strikes my heart. Stories of triumph by the likes of runner Derek Redmond, swimmer Michael Phelps, basketball great Magic Johnson and so many others stir up strong emotions in me. All the great athletes and moments in sports have one thing in common:

they make what seemed impossible possible. They offer us a glimpse of the kind of perfection of which humans are capable.

I remember that day back in 1987 my dad bought hot dogs and popcorn for us to share with each other. He joked with everyone around us. I admired that. He felt free to connect with people and make them feel special. And nobody felt more special than me that day. It was perfect.

The draft was a memorable day for other reasons too, more painful ones. That day came near the end of my consistent contact with my father for the next several years. His presence in my life had already started to wane by the time I was eight, a couple years after my parents divorced. He became less and less present over time until he finally disappeared when I was fifteen. After that he was rarely to be found until sometime in my early twenties.

When I was nine years old I asked my mom if my father was in jail because I hadn't seen or heard from him. I could see the hurt in her eyes as I waited for her response. Without saying much, she packed me up in the car and drove us to Suffolk County, Long Island. It was cold and snowing outside, and I was bundled up in my winter coat. We arrived at a place that looked like a country club, but we had to enter through security gates and check in at the front desk. We waited in the lobby for what seemed like an eternity. Finally, my dad came out from around the corner with a big smile on his face. He always seemed to have a big smile on his face. He opened his arms wide and hugged me.

"Merry Christmas, son," he said.

He looked embarrassed. I didn't really understand it at the time, but I'll never forget that look. It was if his manhood had been taken from him.

My mother consoled me on the way home. She said that my father was getting the help he needed (for his drug addiction, though she didn't tell me that at the time). I was confused as to exactly what was happening, but I knew it wasn't normal. But as we drove home l felt relieved: my father was alive and not in jail. This gave me hope that I'd see him again.

All the same, with the divorce happening when I was six and the visit to my dad in drug rehab on Christmas Day when I was nine, my world started looking a little different. I felt a little less safe and a little lonelier.

For the next few years after the NBA draft, my father did the best he could to show up for my games and events. I remember him being there for some of the biggest games of my life and missing some of the others. Although his visits were sporadic, I always held out hope that he'd show up.

Years later my mother told me what she thought about my heart. She said that during the years my father struggled the most I was the only one in the family who would go check to see how he was doing. I didn't even realize she knew. She told me that she admired how I never gave up on my father. Hearing her say that shifted something in me. Even writing about it now stirs up powerful feelings of empathy and compassion. These days people from all walks of life often tell me that I'm able to connect to them emotionally, from a place of authenticity and compassion. I think this is in part because of my upbringing and my relationship with my dad and the loving support of my mom. All of my experiences were necessary for me to develop into the man, father, son and friend I am today.

I've had to really work on my feelings about my relationship with my father. I had lot of pain there. This work took time and commitment, but I now feel grateful to have reconciled my feelings about my father with who I am today. I see that my past resentments only held me back from being as powerful as I could be.

An old "G" once told me that "Resentments are like peeing on yourself—you walk around and you're the only one who feels it." I love that! So true.

For years I resented my father, even when he was getting help, and even after he'd been clean for years. He'd moved on with his life but meanwhile I was walking around carrying all this pain. Imagine the freedom I felt when I was eventually able to let things go through acceptance, humility, compassion and love.

When I felt let down by my father, my initial emotion wasn't usually anger. It was hurt. I created a story of "justifiable anger," but that anger was almost always a secondary emotion. (The first emotion for most of us in similar situations is usually hurt or fear.) Back when someone hurt me or my feelings, I had a tendency to go from hurt to anger, then anger to vindictiveness. I would want to get back at the person who hurt me by hurting them. It was a vicious cycle led in part by the false beliefs that "Men don't show their emotions," or "You can't hurt me! I'm a man, and I'll show you!"

At the end of the day, hurt people tend to hurt other people, but most of all we hurt ourselves. My work in these areas became vital for my transformation as a person, a parent and a man. It helped me to understand, for example, that one of the reasons I felt there were so many unmet expectations on my father's part when I was growing up was because I had held him up as my idol. I could only make peace with my feelings about this when I could honestly say that throughout the periods of abandonment and drug use, one thing was true: my father did the best he could with the tools he had at the time. This was a transformative realization for me, one that required me to really look at how I saw the world and my father.

Self-awareness takes daily practice. It isn't an "I have arrived" moment. I'd love to tell you that those old feelings about my father never come up, or that I now meditate so much that I float above everything. But that's not real. That's not what happens. Everyone can experience setbacks and revert to old behaviors from time to time. The difference for me today is that I've done enough work on myself to question my limiting beliefs and create the possibility of something new from them.

For example, the day my father called to say he didn't realize it would cost money to get into the NBA draft, I didn't get angry with him. Instead, I created the possibility of showing up for my son, and thanking my father for bringing him to the game, which allowed Justice and I the chance to have a great time together.

Today I stand in the possibility of loving things exactly how they are and not trying to manipulate, control or hurt anyone to create change. This isn't always easy, and if I thought I had to do it every day for the rest of my life, I might feel overwhelmed. That's why freedom for me lies in knowing I only have to do it just for today. It's a one-day-at-a-time practice.

Just for today, I choose life.

Just for today, I choose acceptance.

Just for today, I choose compassion.

Just for today, I choose forgiveness.

Just for today, I choose happiness and freedom!

***

I arrive at my stop and head towards the arena.

Here I am, twenty-five years after my own first NBA draft experience, and about to meet my own son outside the Barclays Center for *his* first draft.

"Thanks for bringing Justice," I say to my father when we see each other. I give him a pound (handshake). "On the way over I was remembering the first time you took me to the draft, twenty-five years ago."

He smiles. "That's right. The 'Mark Jackson' draft."

This simple acknowledgement changes the entire tone of the day not only for me, but also for Justice and my dad. I feel complete and at ease. I shake my dad's hand again and give him a half hug. We say our goodbyes, and he turns to catch the next train back to Queens. Justice and I head toward the ticket window, our spirits high.

We make our way through the metal detectors and towards the concession stand to get something to eat. I order two hamburgers.

"Twenty dollars."

I pause and look at the server in amazement, eyebrows raised. I'm expecting a Happy Meal for the dub ($20) I'm about to drop on these burgers! That's it! Just two burgers! $20?! *I must be getting old*, I say to myself, *because I'm starting to sound like my elders who used to spin stories about when they used tokens for trains and the movies were five cents.*

I joke with the server. "You have to be kidding me! Where's the rest of the meal? No fries? No drink? No nothing? Applebee's gives you two entire meals plus dessert for twenty dollars!"

I am obviously in a losing battle. When I mention to Justice my dream about a Happy Meal for what I'm paying our sever joins in the conversation, laughing and joking with us. It's a cool moment that could've been missed if I wasn't truly present or if I'd really been angry about the price. It might not have happened if I'd been caught up in the story that my father was letting me down again. But this day is about my son.

"You're getting a great deal!" continues the server. "The bun is included!"

We go back and forth a minute more then slide on down the counter to pick up our order. We're astonished. I look back at the server wearing a big smile and quietly mouth the words "thank you." He's given us the two burgers and drinks we've ordered, but he's also thrown in two orders of fries and cheese (for the fries) for free. Justice laughs hysterically, but he's also clearly impressed by the server's generosity.

As we walk away, the server yells out, "Hey man, you guys have a great night. It already looks like you're on your way to having one!"

Indeed we are.

As we walk to our seats, Justice looks at me and says, "Dad, everywhere we go it seems like you know everybody."

"I don't know everybody," I say, "but I try to treat everybody with respect, and everybody likes to laugh a little."

We keep walking and talking. From the smile on his face, I can tell he's enjoyed the exchange.

For me, these human moments are what life is all about. They're the silence between the noise. It might sound like a simple story about a burger to you, but to me it's a teachable moment. My son saw me in my element, having a human exchange not filled with expectations or mistreatment of someone just doing his job. He saw me being present, respecting someone and finding humor in the moment. I hope that as my son gets older and hangs out more with his friends, he remembers what can happen when you treat everyone that same way.

We take the stairs up to our seats. The only section available is 205—the seats about twelve rows away from the top of the building. We called these nosebleed seats back in the day, and for good reason.

I think, *We probably have the worst seats in the house*, but then shake that off. This day is about my son. We squeeze past people to reach our seats and settle in for the draft. In between bites of our burgers and cheese fries, I introduce us to the other fans around us in section 205. I'm sure for some thirteen-year-olds these types of introductions might seem a little bit embarrassing, but Justice seems unfazed. He's open, smiling and energized.

The excitement in the section is palpable. Everyone is donning their team hats: Phoenix Suns, Chicago Bulls, New Jersey Nets and, of course, the most unruly of them all, the Philadelphia 76ers. Philly fans have had a notoriously rowdy reputation ever since their football fans threw snowballs at Santa Claus during an Eagles football game one Christmas.

I finally spot a few New York Knicks fans. We've all had the same look for the last ten-plus years: *Please, can you guys give us some hope this year?*

We even make some new friends visiting from France. They're supporting a few foreign players who are going to be drafted. These guys know more about basketball than most Americans. They're borderline analysts who even know the high-school stats of the players. I ask them if they know what cereal their favorite players ate in the third grade.

Laughing, making jokes and teasing guys about their favorite teams breaks the ice between complete strangers. We're impressed by everyone's knowledge, and they're really cool cats. Of course, because I'm a Knicks fan, most jokes are on me, but I still represent for my team and city.

Justice, on the other hand, is a LeBron James fan, so he's feeling pretty good about himself due to the recent success of his team, the Cleveland Cavaliers. I continue to remind him that he was a Miami Heat fan a few years back when LeBron was on their roster. He doesn't seem concerned about being called a "front runner" and not sticking to one team his entire life like us "old folks."

Every time a player is drafted section 205 starts chanting together, and eventually the whole arena joins us. At one point I glance over at Justice and see a huge smile—pure joy—on his face. He's king for the day. It's all about him and his experience. I imagine I must have worn the same look twenty-five years ago, sitting there with my own father.

Section 205 is having so much fun that we begin taking selfies, which you can probably still see if you search for #section205 on Instagram. Throughout the draft, we make friends, connect with one another and exchange numbers, all within a two-and-a-half-hour timeframe. My son is amazed at the level of connection we're able to make with complete strangers over a common interest. This is the ultimate reminder for me about the gift of being present in the moment. The ticket costs are nothing compared to the shared experience. That is priceless.

As the night wears on into the later rounds, people start leaving the arena. Soon the only people left in the top rows are in section 205. The cleaning crew offers us the chance to move down to the front rows of the arena, but nobody wants to leave. What started out as the worst section has become the most alive, fun, and coolest section in the entire arena. It's so popping that an offer to move right in front of the stage doesn't impress us.

Eventually the staff insists we leave, so we break up and head downstairs. Justice and I spend about forty-five more minutes watching the rest of the second round and then make our way to the exit.

We walk down Flatbush Avenue towards the Long Island Rail Road Atlantic terminal in silence, a comfortable silence.

On the train my son looks me straight in the eyes and says, "Dad, this was the best day of my life."

His words sink directly into my heart. My body shivers with goosebumps, and the warmest feeling you can imagine floods my stomach. These kinds of feelings are nothing new, but every time they come along they're magical. That sense of connection with my children has a unique ability to ignite something in me that words can't describe. It's a love like no other.

I say, "Why was this the best day of your life?"

His answer surprises me. Since he's an avid basketball player and fan, I expect him to talk about the players, the teams and the draft. Instead he starts running down a list of what had happened that day: the funny exchange we'd had with the server over the $10 hamburgers, the people we'd met in section 205, our conversations, our laughter, the stories I'd shared about my childhood and our jokes. In other words, his experience of this being the best day of his life has nothing to do with sports and everything to do with feeling loved, connected, important and acknowledged. It's less about drafts and more about laughs. It's less about the section and more about affection. It's less about teams and more about his dreams. He feels heard, seen and acknowledged in this moment.

I haven't done anything extraordinary. I didn't even spend a lot of money (the tickets for section 205 were only about $30 each). But the memories of this experience will last a lifetime. And Justice will be able to pass this story on to his own children, to share these life lessons about connection, acknowledgment, laughter and more, and create this feeling in his own life.

Basketball had just been a conduit for a deep connection between my son and me. This kind of connection is available to every parent, every day. It can happen at a dance recital or on a simple walk to the store. Being present and connected is one of the greatest gifts we can give our children, because it helps them feel like they're the most important people in our lives.

During that train ride home, it becomes obvious to me again that I could have approached the evening with an outside-in type of thinking, where I thought that the outside world (where our seats were, how much the burgers cost, etc.) would determine our inside world (happiness). Instead we ended up with free fries and the best seats in the house. This is a heartfelt reminder that everything I've been looking for—happiness, connection with my children, wealth and freedom—is an inside job.

THE LEGACY ZONE

Complete the following activity to practice creating and committing to uninterrupted quality time with your children.

ACTIVITY #1: "PRACTICING PRESENCE"

1. Pull out your calendar and pick a day that you will commit to spending quality time with your children.

   - Ask your child what they would like to do (for example, go to the park, take in a game, wrestle, read a book together), or decide together.
   - Be fully present with your child during this time, allowing for connection, laughter and spontaneity, just you and him/her uninterrupted (no cell phone, no book—unless you're reading it aloud—and so on).

2. Ask your child how they enjoyed the time together, and listen for their answer. Ask yourself the same question (and listen for the answer). Make a mental note or journal all the things that made the experience so special. Then take a few moments to see how you can create more experiences like these. If there were things about what happened that you'd like to enhance or improve, make a note of them and see how you can incorporate those ideas moving forward.

3. Pull out the calendar and do it again!

5

WORK-LIFE BALANCE BULLSHIT

Anyone can make the simple complicated.
Creativity is making the complicated simple.

~ Charles Mingus

The phrase "work-life balance" is thrown around in conversations at the dinner table and in companies around the world. Try asking a few people over the next week how work is going, and while I can't claim to predict the future, I'll bet a lot of them will tell you they're "trying to achieve balance."

Seems reasonable, right? With everything we're juggling day-in and day-out, whether we're working in the city or from home, the demands on our time can feel overwhelming. Finding just the right "balance" of work life, home life, social life and so on seems like an admirable goal, doesn't it?

I have a slightly different take on this issue. Let me phrase it as follows:

If I hear another "expert" talk about how they're going to help you achieve work-life balance, I think I'll throw up.

Let's start with the basics. The idea of a "work-life balance" is, by definition, flawed. It implies that you will someday strike a perfect equilibrium between your employer's priorities and your private lifestyle. What will that look like, exactly? I wonder if you've ever heard of…

. . . an employee telling their boss, "I've been working three hours, so now I'm taking a three-hour break to do yoga and Pilates. I need to have balance."

. . . an employer telling their employees, "You know, I know you haven't finished the work to meet that important deadline, but why don't you go home early anyway to make sure you find balance?"

. . . a stay-at-home dad saying to his kid, "Well, son, I've already logged 4.25 hours on home stuff today, so I can't help you with your math homework or I'll fall out of balance."

Even successful entrepreneurs who talk about the freedom they've created in their "four-hour week" often fail to tell you about the sixteen-hour days they logged for years in order to get there.

I mean nothing personal against those who claim you can achieve perfect harmony in your life, but I think we get caught on the hamster wheel of regurgitated rhetoric and it often ends up doing more harm than good.

So, no, I'm not a big fan of the phrase "work-life balance" or the pressure it puts on fathers and parents in general. My experience shows me that the idea that life can be a perfectly balanced seesaw is an illusion. In fact, believing this, and struggling to achieve it, creates stress, unhappiness and a constant search for fulfillment from an outside-in approach. (That is, you think you'll be happy inside if certain conditions are met on the outside.) Day after day too many fathers raise expectations for a "balanced" life only to end their days feeling like failures.

But you *can* create fulfillment in your life and work every day without making it a balancing act. The secret lies in realizing you can make tradeoffs.

In reality it's *all* life, right? Once upon a time someone sold us the idea that we need to separate life into different compartments—work, home, children, play, and so on. But at the end of the day these are *all part of our lives*. As we begin to accept the vision of an integrated life, we start creating a life of possibility—as opposed to a "balanced" life that keeps us juggling and stressed. There is freedom in being okay with knowing that sometimes certain areas of your life will require focused attention and energy. When you realize that one of those moments has arrived, also realize that it isn't a commitment you're making for your entire life. It's an in-the-moment *commitment* to focus on what's most important right then and there.

The concept of work-life balance itself has an underlying message that we need to *find* it before we can have a well-rounded life. But since the whole idea is an illusion, if we keep trying to find it we can gradually become desensitized and fall victim to a mindset that we have no control over our life, family, well-being or happiness.

I'm here to call bullshit on that! I don't want a "well-rounded" life—I want an EXTRAORDINARY life.

I don't want a life by default, shaped by just letting the chips fall where they may. I want a life where I wake up every day energized and committed to the day ahead.

I want a life where I show up BIG as a man, father, business owner, friend, son and game changer in society.

I want a life that is intentionally created based on what I value and love most.

I want my life to be an inspiration for my children so they can see for themselves that they can create an amazing, fulfilling and extraordinary life.

That's what I want. That, and one more thing: I want the same for you.

The only way I've found to truly make an extraordinary life possible is to flip the concept of work-life balance on its head. So today I look at EVERYTHING I do as an intentional choice to do my LIFE'S WORK! Not work-life!

Work doesn't come before life for me. My life's work is all encompassing. I've found a way out of the struggle to find "balance" by creating new strategies to achieve freedom in my life, work, and relationships. The payoff has been my living a simple yet extraordinary life. I travel more than ever. I spend more quality time with my children. I go to their school meetings, fly down from NYC to Florida to visit my daughter in college, and have Knicks basketball season tickets and enjoy games with my children and friends (okay, they're not always enjoyable—depending on how the Knicks are doing). I've created a life that allows me the opportunity to write this book and continue my mission to impact the lives of fathers and families worldwide. I have a life that is joyous and free—truly free.

In creating my life's work I got clear that joy exists in the here-and-now. It is not a destination. My outward success involving money and recognition is only a reflection of my inward success (fulfillment, peace, freedom, love). In other words, balance comes from within. Freedom lies in the successful *integration* of everything in your life (work, home, community, self).

Trust me on this. I was just like some of you. I thought there weren't enough hours in the day to do the things I loved. I thought balance was possible. I thought I could be a great multi-tasker and be everything to everybody. I made myself feel better by saying that freedom, joy, happiness and prosperity would come to me someday.

That day didn't arrive until I intentionally created it. And you can do this too.

Let me take you back to when things were much more hectic in my life. One January morning my alarm clock went off for the third time. I had already hit the snooze button twice. It was Monday. I rolled over in bed and stared at the ceiling. I thought to myself, *I've just got to get through to Friday. Just four more days until Friday.* But the weekends were never long enough. Who was I kidding?

I eventually got out of bed and headed into the bathroom. As I was shaving my head, I looked at myself in the mirror. I saw the face of a man who was physically and mentally exhausted. I wasn't looking forward to work, and I said to myself, *I hate my new job. I'm not doing what I love anymore. I'm not helping people like I used to.*

Once dressed and ready, I grabbed a cup of coffee—there was no time for breakfast—and I headed out to catch the subway into Manhattan. I put my headphones on and listened to some hip-hop to try to awaken my spirit. The music didn't help. I thought about Omari and felt sad. This was the point when his mother and I were going through a divorce, and he was living with her in New Jersey. I thought about my career. I ached to do and be something more. I knew I could, but I didn't know how.

There is so much I want to do and experience, I thought, *but my life is confusing and a bit of a blur. My kids are okay, and I spend a decent amount of time with them. I'm not working twelve-hour days, but I still feel like I'm failing. I know I'm not living up to my own expectations as a man, as a father and as a contributor.*

Once at work it felt like the same old, same old. I had been promoted a few months before but I hated my new job, which was sitting at a desk and calling a network of providers to convince them to partner with our organization. It was another day in my office on the twenty-second floor overlooking 32nd and Broadway.

I thought, *Is this how my life is going to be? Is this it?*

On this particular day one thing, at least, was different. I knew that the following week I was headed to California for a leadership retreat. I checked the weather in Ojai, and daydreamed about the sunshine. I had no clue what to expect. It had only been a handful of days since I'd made the commitment to attend. I'd gone back and forth in my head trying to convince myself that it wasn't a good idea, that it wasn't the right time.

When the retreat had first been offered it sounded great. The organizer said he'd waive the registration fee if I could get a plane ticket and a place to stay. For three days I struggled with what I now call a "scarcity mindset." I could only think of what I didn't have and what I thought wasn't going well in my life. My thinking told me my ex-wife was going to take everything, leaving me broke, eating ramen noodles and homeless, living on the Bowery. Each day I woke up I'd make an excuse as to why I couldn't go.

"There's not enough time to plan."

"The plane ticket's too expensive."

"Will it really be worth it?"

Finally, after the third day of waking up with a pit in my stomach, I came to a realization: if I didn't go I might regret it for the rest of my life. My life and future were on the line. Saying "no" could've meant being resigned to the default life I was living. So I picked up the phone and called up the Lavender Inn in Ojai.

"This is Devon, and it'll be my first time in O-JAY, California."

The lady on the other end laughed hysterically and said, "Devon, you sound like a nice guy, but O.J. is that guy we don't talk about out here. This is O-HI."

We both laughed, and the journey began.

Nine days later I arrived in California to sunshine and "winter" temperatures in the sixties. I'd left New York's snow and 17° weather behind.

This was the first time in a long time that I'd taken a break from the rat race and could rest. As the days passed, I was able to give myself space, attention and time to focus on my life and figure out where I was—and where I was going.

One day in particular stands out to me the most. Though I didn't know it at the time, it was the day my life began to change. That change also began to impact my children's future.

The retreat facilitator and one of my first mentors, Jason Womack, asked the following two questions:

What do you have 10,000 hours of experience in?
What would you do as a career if money weren't an issue?

My answers were instant: fatherhood and leadership coaching.

I had extensive experience developing fatherhood programs for the non-profit organization I worked for, not to mention my own experiences and journey as a father. There was no question that I'd contributed far more than 10,000 hours to fatherhood. More importantly, for me fatherhood was an incredibly joyful experience. Being a father is so fulfilling, and it brings out the best in me.

As for coaching, I realized I had been doing this most of my life. I started out coaching youth basketball teams when I was fifteen. This morphed into "coaching" individuals like Sean in my first job after college. Eventually I coached a team of social workers as a director of a non-profit organization. Running the fatherhood programs, mentoring and coaching people was (and is) what I loved most—not trying to convince a network of providers to partner with our non-profit organization.

I shared my answers with my mentor, and he said, "Then build a business around that."

"What?" I said. "Build a business around the things I love most and would do for free? No way! Is that even a thing?"

He nodded "yes," with a smirk that indicated he'd been there and done that. He knew it was possible.

This was the start of a new opportunity for me. Although the answers to those two questions had come easily, my mind quickly jumped in and got in the way. I immediately shifted from a world of possibilities into the "how-to's." I asked myself,

How am I going to create a business around this?

How am I going to find the time?

How am I going to make enough money?

We wrapped up the leadership retreat in a room atop what they called "Meditation Mountain." Jason asked us to reflect on our weekend experiences, and even as I did so my mind started throwing out more questions:

Is this the right time with the divorce going on?

Will it ever be the right time?

What if I fail?

What if I am hugely successful?

What if I could actually do this?

When Jason asked us to focus on our purpose, mission and our "why," I calmed myself and sat quietly, journal in hand, looking out over the cloud-covered mountains of California.

Then the answers to my questions began to emerge.

Normally my life was constantly masked by noise disguised as busyness—the busyness of my everyday life, my commitments and competing priorities. And the noise of self-doubt—so loud at times that it sounded like the roar of five o'clock traffic and crowded subway cars. But on top of Meditation Mountain I experienced once again the quiet confidence and understanding that everything I had experienced in my life to date was necessary. All of it.

I also felt that this understanding came to me at the exact time it was supposed to. It wasn't meant to come any earlier, and it wasn't meant to come without struggles. Every experience in my life had prepared me to take this next step and create an intentional life that I loved, one that impacted the people around me.

In that moment of clarity I felt free, inspired, and calm.

The decision to attend the leadership retreat in Ojai changed everything for me. It was the first time in a long while that I felt like myself again. I had slowed down to the speed of life. This was an amazingly subtle yet enormous shift in my perspective. It became one of the tenets of a philosophy that I eventually came to call my "Life's Work."

Before I knew it the retreat was over and it was time to go home. On the plane ride back to NYC, I reflected on the weekend. I felt re-energized, re-focused and excited about the possibilities for my life. I had a plan for how to launch my new business, and I was hopeful about it.

Granted, I *still* wondered if it were really possible. It seemed like a HUGE, audacious goal to build a business while working full-time, helping raise three children and going through a divorce. My circumstances on the outside hadn't changed, but on the inside I was a completely different person.

That said, I'll never forget the day when I shared with a friend my dream of having a business where I traveled around the world helping others. He turned to me and said, "You can't do that! Build a business where you travel so much? You have three kids!"

The words stung. A lot. For a hot minute I doubted myself and thought, *Is this really possible? Can I really do this?*

I did my best to ignore my friend and follow the plan. I created a daily routine to stay on track and followed up on all the actions that could bring me closer to my goals. I blocked out time to read, start a blog and do research. I reached out to other successful coaches and speakers to ask about their experiences and journey. Things started coming together, and before I knew it I caught a wave of momentum.

I found my zone!

I began to truly understand: we don't have to live a life of either/or. We can live a life of AND.

In just a few short years after the retreat, I traveled more than ever AND I spent more time with my children than I had at any other time in my life. My business has been successful beyond my wildest dreams. It feels amazing! I work with great people and businesses, AND I have time to do the things I value the most. My life has become simpler AND fuller at the same time. I've made more money than ever before, AND it hardly feels like work. At least not like the work I had grown accustomed to in the past.

Ever since that day on top of Meditation Mountain I've never again dreaded waking up and going to work.

Following the retreat, I had a mission and a purpose. I would come home from work and spend time and be more present with my children. Later in the evening I would focus on building my business. In the mornings I was off to work, this time for a greater good. I wanted to permanently change the national conversation around fatherhood through my coaching and speaking. The days of low energy and high fatigue became fewer and fewer. My days were filled with excitement, focus and creativity. Don't get me wrong: it was hard work, but it was also fulfilling. And that's what made it so great.

My twelve-month plan came to fruition within nine months of the retreat when I stepped on stage to give my own TEDx Talk. I had already established a fatherhood podcast, and requests to speak around the country started coming in. My coaching practice was growing, and each day brought me closer to fully transitioning into the full-time CEO of the Devon Bandison Company.

This all started with an idea—and a challenge—to leave the "safe" world behind and set out into uncharted territory. My decision required me to make trade-offs and create intentionality in my days. I didn't have work-life balance. I integrated my Life's Work into all aspects of living. I integrated everything I love (my children, family, business, and work) into my days, weeks and months. I didn't make time for things that didn't align with what I valued most.

The decision was life-altering, and it helped me create the freedom, joy and prosperity I enjoy today. The biggest reward hasn't been all the great things that have happened to me. It's been the impact my decisions have had on my children, my family, my friends, my clients and my community—which I serve every day.

THINK ABOUT A JAZZ QUARTET

Let's take a look at how best to create your Life's Work, where every day you can wake up excited, energized and on purpose.

All the successful people I know never accomplished anything great by themselves. In my conversations with true game changers, I've learned that their success included learning from and being mentored or coached by others. I am no different. This kind of collaborative learning approach has been a staple of my success. So many people on my path have helped make my transition fun and fulfilling. In fact, I still continue my journey with my own coach, and by reading books, taking online courses, scheduling conversations with people I admire and more—all as part of my learning process.

One person who's had a significant impact on my journey is Stew Friedman, a gentleman I interviewed for my podcast, *Fatherhood is Leadership*. Stew is a professor at the University of Pennsylvania Wharton School of Business. He's also the Founding Director of the Wharton Leadership Program and Wharton's Work/Life Integration Project. Stew is the real deal, a genuine human being and someone you want to learn more about the moment you meet him. His book and online program, both called *Total Leadership*, were game changers for me.

When I interviewed him, Stew described what he calls "work-life integration"—the successful blending of home and work life, community and self. He uses an analogy for this type of life that I'll never forget.

Life and its quadrants are, he says, like a jazz quartet. In a jazz quartet there are different instruments, such as a saxophone, bass, trombone and drums. Sometimes the drummer has a solo, and the other instruments fade into the background. Sometimes it's the bass or trombone or sax that's featured. But they're all vital for creating amazing music.

The same holds true with your life's work. Sometimes you have trade-offs. Work may be the current soloist and require more of your attention. Another time it'll be home, yourself or your community.

Now in order for you to create a life of freedom and abundance you first have to identify which instruments you're playing with. Mine include:

- Fatherhood (home)

- Building a dream business (work)

- Traveling (self)

- The calling to help people create miracles in their lives (community)

This is my jazz quartet. This is how I play my own beautiful music of life.

I created a life around the things that I value most. You won't find me hanging in the club, lounge or after-hours spots—not because that's bad (it's all good if that's your thing!), but because that's just not what I value in my life. That is not one of my instruments.

PULL OUT THE FEATHER

Fathers, take a step back and give yourselves a break. Realize that the circumstances in your life right now are the result of the tools you're using. There is no reason to beat yourself up. That doesn't serve you. It only takes you down a rabbit hole of self-loathing that will ensure you're not at your best. Take a look at your tools, systems and mindset, and make adjustments. Hopefully this book will help with that, too. But stay in the game. Remember: your situation is not your destination.

If you choose any form of punishment I suggest you put down the baseball bat and pick up a feather instead. When I work with high-performing athletes, the ones who are most clutch (as opposed to being likely to choke) in stressful situations are the ones who aren't uptight because of the mistakes they've made. One professional basketball player with whom I was working as a life coach was fond of saying that if he misses ten shots in a row, he knows the eleventh one is going in. That's an important lesson in parenting and life. Keep taking the shots, stay on the court and have confidence that the next one will go in.

REALIZE THAT "NO" IS A COMPLETE SENTENCE

One of the biggest struggles working fathers have involves their inability to say no. We worry about coming across as rude. We wonder if we'll sour a relationship by saying "no" to an invitation that isn't one of our priorities. We end up saying "yes" to things we don't value at the expense of the things we do. This is why we never "have time."

Think about it: maybe your problem isn't so much about time management as it is about people-pleasing and a lack of intentionality and focus in your life.

Start saying "yes" to the things you value. If time with your children is important, then why haven't you spent any with them in two weeks? If going to the gym is important then why haven't you lifted weights in months?

We have to intentionally create time in our day for the things we value. This means cutting away the things we don't value, at least not as highly.

One of the greatest lessons I learned about saying "no" was this: "No" is a complete sentence. "No" doesn't need an explanation. Saying it doesn't make you arrogant. It doesn't mean that you don't honor commitments. It simply means you're choosing what's best for you and your family. When you say "no" to something you don't value much, you are actually saying "YES" to things you do value.

Let me share an example of this process. It was in the midst of the divorce and Omari was living with his mother. I had just launched my speaking/coaching career and had dreams of speaking all over the world. You'll recall from the beginning of the book my Friday Night Pizza Night with Omari. We had just started this ritual, and it was important because I wanted him to know how special he was and that the divorce wasn't his fault. So I was committed to keeping this date free.

But within two months of launching my business I received a call from a conference organizer out in California. It was the ONE conference I'd always wanted to speak at. I couldn't believe the opportunity had come so soon! This was a gig that would place me in front of thousands of people whom I could serve well beyond my speech. It would be an opening into something much bigger for my career. The organizer told me how excited they were to have me speak and shared with me how much I'd be compensated. WOW! It was the largest fee I'd ever been offered, AND it was for a dream conference opportunity. I asked her to send over the contract for me to sign.

When I opened the email, I had butterflies, but an instant later my stomach dropped.

I was scheduled to speak on a Friday night.

So I had a decision to make. I could take this amazing opportunity, one that would surely benefit my business, or I could honor my commitment to Omari. It only took a few moments of contemplation. Omari was my number one priority at the moment, and we were only a few months into our pizza ritual. I knew he was feeling especially vulnerable lately. Maybe there would be a time in the future when cancelling would be okay—when I could give the talk AND still support my son—but now wasn't that time. I had to choose which instrument in my quartet got the solo.

There was no real decision to make.

I picked up the phone and called the organizer, thanked her for the opportunity and respectfully declined. When I said it was because I had a family commitment, the organizer said she understood. But her tone told a different story, one mixed with confusion. It might have been the first time someone turned down such a gig. I thanked her again, saying I hoped we'd stay in touch and that another opportunity for me to be of service would arise in the future. Then I hung up the phone. Pizza Night has continued for three years straight. Eventually I was able to take a Friday commitment here and there. But in the early stages of our Friday night ritual, establishing that I was there for Omari was my first priority.

I didn't have a "time-management" problem. I wasn't being pulled in different directions by competing priorities. I simply made a decision based on the things I value most, and it was simple to do. Since then I've been offered many more opportunities to speak around the world, and my business has grown tenfold. My son and I still have our Friday Night Pizza Night.

Sometimes saying "no" is the path to freedom in life.

THE LEGACY ZONE

This section will help you clarify what you value most and establish priorities around it. It's time to be selfish here. The benefit of this form of self-care is that it allows you to reboot, re-energize and recommit to yourself. The better you treat yourself, the better you will show up in the world for others.

1. Take out a piece of paper and write out the ideal "Fatherhood Job Description" as you see it. (Extra credit: also have your child write out your job description.) For example: "I want to be the type of father who experiences what it feels like to spend five hours a week with my child, make it home in time for dinner with the family each night, create "me" time to go to the gym three times a week and hang with the guys twice a month."

2. Create a personal mission and vision statement for your life's work.

3. Now review and compare #1 and #2, and from those responses take time to reflect on what you value most in your life.

4. Write down the specific experiences you would like to create for yourself and in your home, work, and community over the next twelve months.

5. Pull out your calendar and look over the next thirty days. What are you committed to building into your calendar based on what you've discovered? For example: "I commit to going to the gym one time this week, on Monday [put it

on your calendar]. I commit to going to the park for one hour on Saturday [put it on your calendar]," and so on.

REFLECTION

Write about your experiences in your journal for the next thirty days.

1. What did you learn about yourself while completing the exercise?

2. What opportunities are now available for you that weren't available before?

3. What are you no longer willing to compromise in order to have a fulfilling life?

6

THE MAN IN THE MIRROR

There's no need to be perfect to inspire others. Let people get inspired by how you deal with your imperfections.

~ Ziad K. Abdelnour

Does your audio match your video?

Let me ask you that same question a different way: does what you say match what you do?

This is one of my favorite questions to live by. To me it represents a shift away from the old way of doing things and into modern-day fatherhood. Many of us were raised by parents whose authoritarian parenting style didn't allow much space for us to have a say—or even a thought—of our own. An authoritarian parenting style is fear-based. It's based on a belief that parenting works best when children are afraid of their parents. I believe this approach is ineffective over time. What's more, it negatively impacts the opportunity for parents and children to form one of the most enriching bonds of their lives. But it's still used by many parents today.

"Do as I say, not as I do" is a common approach with this style of parenting. When I first became a parent I initially bought into the hype. But the notion that our children should shut up and "just do it" only works if we're in a Nike commercial or are tyrants in a third-world country. It won't work if we want to raise the next generation of leaders.

I've heard variations on the following thought with many people: "The way we were brought up worked out just fine. Look at how we turned out!" (Sometimes I want to respond with something like: "Yeah, look how we turned out—so many of us struggling with basic self-esteem issues, struggling to believe in our own strength, dealing with broken relationships, and so on.") If this is the way you feel, I invite you to stay open to what we're talking about here. Like I said above, I too once bought into this myth that hard-nosed discipline and punishment were the answers. But research has shown that children don't actually develop better when they receive corporal punishment. In fact, children raised in an authoritarian household are, in the long term, more prone to antisocial behavior, increased aggression and mental health issues. So, really, sticking to the "good old" days and ways of parenting is like sticking to cigarettes because back in the day they were touted as safe and cool.

As fathers we need to realize that children watch our every move. Because of this, what we do is at least as important as what we say. Sending children the message that what you say doesn't need to match what you do is just plain played out. The best way to teach anyone, at home or at work, is by modeling.

I once asked a father who tried to stop his thirteen-year-old from cursing if he himself cursed in front of his child. He said, "I'm the adult. It shouldn't matter."

"Okay," I replied. "Well, it does matter, and that's why we're having this conversation. Are you open to trying something new?"

My son Justice reminded me to check if my audio matched my

video one weekend when he was fourteen. He and Omari were roughhousing like they always do, and they were having a great time. I encourage my sons to play together and often participate in the roughhousing myself. This particular day, however, I wasn't in the mood to hear and see all that. I really wanted time to think. I had a deadline for an important proposal and was struggling to put it together. Suddenly I reached a tipping point and it was like a bomb went off. I yelled, "Cut the shit!"

They stopped roughhousing immediately. There was a hard silence, during which I saw the shock and awe in my sons' eyes. They've come to know me as a pretty mild-mannered parent, but today was clearly different.

After a few minutes, Justice sheepishly said, "Dad, can I ask you a question?"

Knowing that Justice and I have similar personalities, I braced myself for a comment that would either push me more over the edge or bring levity to the situation.

I said, "Yes."

"What kind of fatherhood-is-leadership is that?"

I looked at him. He stared back.

Then all three of us burst into uncontrollable laughter.

If I had been a "back-talk, back-hand" type of parent, that wouldn't have happened. But we had a great moment together. I realized that over the years I had cultivated a relationship with Justice such that he could ask me that question. And even in the midst of something that seemed so tense, Justice recognized I was off my game and found a way to bring me back. He taught me that children are always listening and watching. My audio wasn't matching my video, and he pointed it out.

I acknowledged my mistake and we enjoyed the rest of the weekend. This is another thing: the ability to admit when I'm wrong has been a powerful life lesson afforded to me by fatherhood. One of the greatest messages I can offer my children is that I'm not perfect and that I don't expect them to be perfect. I tell them to do their best, and to correct course and move on when they fall short of it.

So I do the same thing.

This approach will also help you if you're a boss, leader, co-worker or spouse. Too many people hold themselves up to unrealistic, perfectionistic standards, only to realize that they're human and will fall short now and again. For my own part, accepting this has brought greater freedom to my life. It has also transformed the lives of the fathers and people I coach.

Underneath this need to look perfect and not admit our mistakes lies something more. This "thing" make us inflexible and tricks us into needing control in all situations. It makes us procrastinate, settle for less, take alcohol and drugs or become sick with fear.

All of us experience fear in one way or another. Whether it's fear of failure, fear of success, fear of being alone or fear of letting someone down. Fear can become paralyzing. If we let it, fear can keep us from becoming the best versions of ourselves. In exploring these issues with my clients I have seen that everything usually comes down to two particular fears:

1. We're not enough

2. We won't be (or don't deserve to be) loved

Now most men won't admit to feeling either of these things, because our hardwiring from years of societal conditioning reinforces old stereotypes that:

1. Real men don't need help. ("I'm afraid I'll look weak.")

2. Real men can't be vulnerable. ("I'm afraid I'll be taken advantage of or not be respected.")

3. Real men are breadwinners and don't have time for household stuff. ("I'm afraid I'll be seen as less of a man.")

4. Real men NEVER admit they're wrong. ("I'm afraid I'll lose respect.")

When I see a father acting out any of these outdated beliefs, I see a scared little boy behind it all. I was once that scared little kid, too, pretending like nothing was wrong and that I was invincible. This is all a front, and it can keep men locked in self-made prisons for years. And even when they can admit to themselves that they've got a problem, most men refuse to ask for help. I witnessed this firsthand in my group work with fathers. It normally took at least a session or two for men to take off their masks and open up.

As men, we try to figure out everything on our own. We put on a mask of invincibility—and end up suffering in silence. Even if someone offers help, we greet them with the conventional, "I'm good. I'll figure it out."

Figure what out? Life? Parenting? Human behavior? Just like that?

C'mon, think about the standard you're setting for yourself. We're not perfect, and we don't need to act like we are. Fathers, when it feels like you need this tight grip of control, understand that you're operating from a fear-based mindset. It won't serve you in the long run.

Of course, in the short term there's a benefit to this way of thinking. That's why we keep doing it. We need to acknowledge this payoff in order to move past it. For example, my fear often played itself out by making me think I needed to control everything and act like I had it all together. The payoff was that I was able to keep people at distance and be left alone. I felt comfortable—and lonely. So I struggled for years but couldn't ask for help without breaking down the barrier I'd set up between myself and others. It was only when I took a deeper look that I saw how the short-term benefits would lead to negative long-term consequences.

One of my clients grew up with a father who feared she would be a failure. So he pushed and pushed her to follow the family professional path and become a doctor. She obliged, although her true passion lay in the creative arts. She found the journey torturous, but she never questioned her father because he was above reproach. At age thirty-five, after practicing medicine for a few years, she was depressed and lonely, and she found that she resented her father—whom she hadn't spoken to in years.

Now his intentions had been good, but his fear that his daughter's success was a reflection of his legitimacy as a father created a wedge between them. The long-term damage in both their lives was evident. Our work together created the space for them to reconcile, and she eventually changed her career. This work started when the father was able to reveal that his intentions, while pure in his mind, were based in the fear that his daughter wouldn't amount to anything, which in turn would mean that he wasn't a good father.

None of this was true. But all of the stories we create can lead to serious consequences, such as separations and grievances within families. Our fear can have reverberating effects on everyone around us.

So what happens when your children fail? You know they will, over and over again. Do you see their failure as a sign of your own failure as a parent? Answer that question honestly, and see how it may be coloring your decision-making as a parent.

One question a lot of fathers ask me is this: "How did you become such a great father and learn to navigate it all?"

The first time someone asked me this I was surprised. The question implies that I *know* how to "navigate it all"—which I don't. But I honor this question every time I hear it. I understand that in general it's hard for men to ask for help and admit they need guidance.

Maybe these men see the time I spend with my children and assume it's always a smooth ride. As I've pointed out, it's not! Yes, I am blessed to have wonderful, fun, challenging, loving and creative relationships with my children. I wouldn't change that for the world. But creating that dynamic took work. In fact it's still a continual process of growth for both my children and me. I fall short, they fall short—and by doing so we learn some of life's greatest lessons together.

So when I see a man reaching out, breaking through the "man box" and asking for my help, I receive it with special attention and compassion. I know how hard it is for us men to ask for help.

Over time my answer to the question about navigating it all has evolved into what's probably the most honest and straightforward one I can give: I've improved as a father because I constantly search for growth and opportunity in failure.

I use the word "failure" loosely, because to me it has come to mean just another way for the universe to show me I still have room to grow. I understand that in the moment, when we've really messed up, it feels like failure. But that's only temporary. My fear of failure has lessened every time I lean into my edge—every time I challenge myself to find that line in me where fear of failure lies—then stretch past it.

I can honestly say that fear of failure is not a major part of my life. Because of this I can now show up knowing that I am enough, that I can be me no matter where I am. This allows me to say "no" when I want to say "no" without fearing what people will think of me. It allows me to make tough decisions as a parent, decisions that I know come from a loving place in my heart, even when my children don't agree with them.

This is the path to freedom.

The thought that someone has this fatherhood thing all figured out is ridiculous. I've made a ton of errors including, but not limited to: putting work before home, taking out my frustrations on my children by yelling and cursing, not spending enough time with them, spanking, breaking promises and sometimes not being kind to their mothers. I'm not proud of these things, but I admit they're the very things that have helped me transform my life as a man and as a father. I couldn't do this if I never admitted I was wrong, or if I let myself be crushed by failure.

It's from these moments that I've learned how to better love my children, their mothers, the world—and most of all myself. When we inevitably fall short of perfectionistic expectations, what typically follows is a series of internal judgments about our behavior—thoughts like "I'm not good enough," "I'm a bad person," or "I'm a bad father, spouse, or friend." It's a bitter cycle into the land of victimhood. But once we accept that we're human, that we will fail at times, we don't need to judge ourselves that way.

Fathers, be open to making mistakes and learning from them. Let your guard down and face your fears. The best advice I can give is to be okay with your humanness. You don't need to have all the answers and you don't need to be perfect. Just do the best you can in the here and now with the information you have. There will always be more information, new perspectives and learning opportunities. Start where you stand in your humanness and most authentic self.

As my coach Steve Chandler reminds me, authenticity isn't something you create. When I approach my living room ready to play with my six-year-old, I don't stop to ask myself, "How can I be authentic?" I just go into the room, roll around on the floor and say whatever comes to mind. Authenticity is a natural place to come from, not somewhere to get to.

***

When I served as Director of Children's Services for a non-profit agency in NYC, my role included oversight of the South Bronx First-Time Fatherhood Program. This program supported fathers ages thirteen to thirty-five (yes you read that right: thirteen) in developing the skills necessary for becoming better men and fathers. These guys were from the South Bronx, a tough area historically ranked in the top three most poverty-stricken areas in the country. The South Bronx is known for a host of psychosocial and environmental issues, such as 50 percent high-school dropout rates and prevalent drug addiction, single-parent households, emotional/physical abuse, neglect, and trauma. I would go as far as saying that everyone growing up in this neighborhood is exposed to trauma. Even young kids are likely to encounter traumatic events when simply walking or taking the bus home from school.

What I loved about working with the men in this program is that they made the decision to break with cultural norms and ask for help. Their definition of a "real man" was exactly the same as that of my clients who seemingly "had it all"—the CEOs, professional athletes, entrepreneurs, and so on. For all of them, "real men" never show emotions. Real men solve problems by showing who's stronger (violence). Real men don't cry. Real men focus on making money and being breadwinners. Real men know success is based on status. And so on and on.

Over the years the men in the South Bronx Fatherhood Program and I did some powerful work, which resulted in recognition across the city. Participants improved their lives socially, emotionally and financially. Ultimately they learned to shift their perspective on what a real man is, and they became powerful examples to their families. They opened up to ask for help, shared their vulnerabilities and took ownership of their roles in their children's and families' lives—financially and emotionally.

Once the internal work was underway through shifting mindsets, habits and behaviors, their outside worlds began to change. Some of the men went on to get their GEDs and college degrees. Others were able to build healthier relationships with their partners. Others started making an impact on the community by helping young people develop healthier lifestyles.

I absolutely loved this work. The transformations these men made were amazing. Moreover, we always talked about the legacy they were creating. The impact of these fathers went well beyond our groups in that conference room in the South Bronx. They affected, and will continue to affect, their children, their children's children and the generations to follow. Why? Because they were breaking the cycle of misguidance and misinformation and creating a new legacy.

***

A few years after I moved on I returned to my old stomping grounds in the South Bronx and paid a visit to the fatherhood program.

I stepped off the 5 train one evening. The air smelled of sweet plantains, and salsa music blasted from an apartment balcony.

When I walked into the conference room I only recognized a few faces. Everyone else was new. I took a moment to settle in. The table by the back wall was stocked with Domino's pizza and soda. Within minutes everything was familiar again.

Now these men knew I had planned on stopping by to give a talk, and they'd done their homework on me. These days everyone can find out about anyone via social media. So when I introduced myself to the group, the guys started letting me know what they knew about me.

"Hey man, I saw your TED talk."

"I saw that TV interview you did."

"I heard your interview on Wu Tang Radio."

"I read that article you wrote."

I felt a little amazed at the level of recognition.

My journey has taught me many things, but one thing's for certain. All of the fathers I've been fortunate enough to work with, coach and help—no matter where they came from, no matter how much or how little they owned or who they knew—had this in common: a beautiful connection to the joy of fatherhood that emanates from the heart and reverberates in the spirit. It's the unexplainable feeling you've probably had yourself when you hold your child. Some men may experience only a glimpse of this in a passing moment. Some get to experience it every day. But that special feeling that reaches the heart is what most fathers share. Whenever I show up at an event I never forget that I'm just another father trying to figure it out. No matter what label people put on me as a "fatherhood expert" or public figure, the reality is that I'm just another father on the journey towards growth and contribution. For me it's important to keep that up front: I'm a father just like you.

Nonetheless, I could tell these guys were expecting a lot of me, even though I was the same guy who'd been the head of this program just a few years ago—not "The Guy!" they were insisting I was now. I was quietly amused and appreciative, but at the same time something felt off. I paused a moment and thought about the message that was emerging from my spirit.

What I didn't want was for this night to be some kind of lecture from me to them. This would have been in direct contrast to my definition of leadership. Leadership, like fatherhood, is about influence, and I suddenly realized I had an amazing opportunity to influence the conversation on this Tuesday night in the boogie-down Bronx.

I decided to scrap the talk I'd planned to give. Instead I sat down on the edge of the table in the front of the room, one leg dangling above the floor, and opened the conversation like this:

"My daughter is away at college. She hasn't spoken to me in

three weeks, and I'm feeling bad about it. I need your guys' help. Who has some ideas of what I should do?"

This changed everything. In a matter of seconds their entire demeanor changed. They started spitting out ideas, started sharing their own struggles. The conversation took off like we were outside waiting for a bus to Yankee Stadium.

What had happened was that they'd let me down from the pedestal they'd put me on and started seeing me as no different from them. As a result my one question turned into a two-hour conversation. By modeling vulnerability and putting my humanness on display, I was able to empower the men to open into conversation with me and share what was going on for them. This allowed for some amazing transformations to occur. These men fought through their fears *by admitting them*—and then leaned into them. As a result, they left ready to go back into the world as different fathers, men and leaders.

A universal truth became clear: men are being misinformed and set up for a fall. We need to challenge the definition of what a "real man" is. What's clear from my work with men and fathers is that those who choose to be themselves, to stand for their values without apology, are stronger emotionally and mentally. And through their leadership they accomplish more in their lives.

For me, this major shift in how I parent has also shifted how I live my life. Our parents did the best they could with the information they had, but now it's our turn, and it's important to realize how things can be different. It's time to step up, find your voice and be the best person you can be. When we're on a pedestal we lack real connection with our children and the world. When was the last time you met someone who acted like they were perfect? Did that inspire you? It's the same with us as fathers. Embrace your failures and realize they represent opportunities to be great fathers. This is leadership. In fact, it's the highest form of leadership—the kind that has great potential to inspire others. As fathers we have the greatest and most fulfilling leadership role in the world. Our actions can positively impact our children and leave a legacy for years to come.

Step up and step into your most authentic self. You are the epitome of greatness. Own it. Take a look in the mirror. Make your word really stand for something.

Live a life where your audio matches your video.

"It is not the critic who counts; not the man who points out how the strong man stumbles, or where the doer of deeds could have done them better. The credit belongs to the man who is actually in the arena, whose face is marred by dust and sweat and blood; who strives valiantly; who errs, who comes short again and again, because there is no effort without error and shortcoming; but who does actually strive to do the deeds; who knows great enthusiasms, the great devotions; who spends himself in a worthy cause; who at the best knows in the end the triumph of high achievement, and who at the worst, if he fails, at least fails while daring greatly, so that his place shall never be with those cold and timid souls who neither know victory nor defeat."

~ Theodore Roosevelt

THE LEGACY ZONE

Following are some approaches that have helped me and my clients overcome fear of failure. For the next thirty days, give one or more a try.

1. **Own your mistakes:** Examine at least one "failure" or mistake this week. Own it, admit you've made it and share it with someone. (For example: *I shouldn't have lost my temper and taken it out on you.*)

2. **Identify contradictions:** Write down your definition of a "real" man followed by your definition of a "good" man. Do they match? Do you notice any old outdated beliefs that you've been holding on to? Are any of these beliefs your parents' and not yours? Name any specific fears you have about what doing or seeing things differently means to you.

3. **Question your beliefs**: When you're struggling or faced with a difficult situation, ask yourself: is this really true? Or is it just a thought? Questioning your thoughts and fears (e.g., fear of losing your job, or your temper with your child, etc.) allows for new alternatives to emerge.

4. **Ask for help:** Open up to a friend or your spouse. Hire a coach. Find a mentor. Ask them to help you challenge your fear-based thinking and bring out the best in yourself.

5. **Focus on gratitude:** Take five minutes a day to look in the mirror. Appreciate and honor yourself as a father. Let the practice of love emerge. Love is the antidote to fear. When fear arises, go to this place and ask "What would love do?" Then do that.

7

DEATH AT 35,000 FEET

If today were the last day of my life,
would I want to do what I'm about to do today?

~ Steve Jobs

I sat in the second to last row of the airplane, terrified, gripping each armrest and thinking:

This is it. My final day on Earth. It was a great ride.

I knew when I became an international speaker and transformational life coach that flying from city to city would be part of the job. I was okay with that. And in the first two years of my new career I flew from New York to California to Portland to Chicago and other places in between, including Utah—probably the last place a New Yorker like me thought he'd be visiting. My travels have sometimes felt like that old Sade song, "Smooth Operator," where she sings, "Coast-to-coast from LA to Chicago." (Now that I think of it, that's not really coast to coast is it? To think I'd been singing it all these years without noticing. Well that's for another day—it's all good.)

In 2016 I took one of my favorites trips: my first event on the West Coast. It was a special time and a monumental week. I had been asked to speak at conferences in California before, but this was the first time I'd held an intensive seminar for a group of leaders. We had parents, CEOs, authors, entrepreneurs and even the founders of the Los Angeles City Dad's Group. (The City Dads started out as a group composed mainly of stay-at-home dads but it has evolved into a movement of support for fathers around the country. As a single father myself, they have a special place in my heart.) We even had a special guest appearance from one of my good friends, Stella Reid, also known as Nanny Stella from the TV series *Nanny 911*. It was an amazing day.

That trip stood out to me as special because of a promise I'd made three years earlier during the leadership retreat I attended in Ojai, California. That was the start of the Devon Bandison Company. As I mentioned in Chapter 5, during that retreat I laid out a plan to create the life I wanted for my family and myself. Three years later, I was living that dream, standing tall as the man, father, son, friend, partner and business owner I could only imagine back then. Out of sincere gratitude for that transformative retreat, I promised that if I ever had a chance to offer a similar leadership experience to others, I would take it. Two-and-a-half years after the retreat, I had done just that. Life seemed to have come full circle.

But it almost didn't happen.

Three months earlier, in April of 2016, I was flying from San Antonio to New York. I'd been attending a three-day coaching retreat sponsored by my coach, Steve Chandler. It had been an amazing fusion of learning, business, fun and joy. Steve is one of the most extraordinary, authentic, non-judgmental and loving men I know. He's been such a big part of my development as a person and as a professional coach. For three weekends out of the year, forty amazing coaches get together to learn from each other. We share with each other how we can best serve out in the world and show up more powerfully for our clients. Each weekend is a wonderful experience that always leaves me feeling inspired and purposeful. In addition, this past weekend my writing coach and editor, Kristi, had flown in from Los Angeles to meet me for lunch with Maurice, the publisher of this very book.

Now by this time flying had become so routine that I'd developed routines for my routine of flying, if you know what I'm saying. I book the first early morning flight out because there are fewer delays and it gives me the entire day ahead once I've landed. I fly the same airline, JetBlue, special circumstances aside. I reserve an aisle seat in keeping with my goal to stay well hydrated—which of course means frequent trips to the bathroom. I even listen to the in-flight safety instructions every time I fly.

My routines calm me to the point where even a little turbulence won't bother me. In fact, turbulence and the occasional runway backup seem quite normal. But there was nothing normal about my early-morning flight in 2016 from San Antonio to New York City.

My routine was thrown from the start that day, but I tried not to let it bother me. I'd booked the first flight out, but I wasn't flying my preferred airline. I didn't have an assigned seat until a few minutes before takeoff, and I ended up sitting in the very last row of the airplane—the only benefit was that I was close to the bathroom. But I settled in, excited to return home.

We sat on the tarmac of the San Antonio airport for about thirty-five minutes, rain pouring down, waiting for takeoff. Passengers seemed to be in a relatively good mood, which seemed par for the average Texan's demeanor. If this were NYC and we'd been waiting over half an hour, you'd best believe there'd be some attitude on the plane! Eventually the captain came on the loudspeaker and told us to expect turbulent weather during our flight. His voice seemed nervous and shaky, and his lack of confidence made me uneasy. I had no idea at the time that the area was about to be slammed with crazy rainfall, which would cause severe flooding throughout that part of Texas.

As we finally taxied towards the runway I tried to get back to normal by fastening my seat belt, checking my phone one last time and saying a quick prayer to the universe to look out.

Once we were up in the air, everything seemed normal. But just as we reached our cruising altitude of 35,000 feet the airplane began to shake violently up and down—it was no match for the stormy weather. It felt like we were in the midst of a battle and the storm was winning. Babies were eerily quiet from fear. Adults were screaming. A few overhead storage bins popped open and bags started falling out, hitting people on the way down. The intercom went silent, and the TV screens went dark.

The airplane seemed to be in its final descent, and I don't mean in preparation for landing.

This was unlike anything I had ever experienced. Everything was out of my control. I felt scared and helpless. I turned my head toward the back of the airplane where a flight attendant sat clutching her seat. Instinctively, I looked to her for comfort, but her face seemed to say all that could be said. She was pale, her mouth tight, hands clutching her seat as if she were going to be launched out of a James Bond-style passenger seat after pressing the ejection button.

I asked her, "Is this normal?!"

She paused before answering. She was young and wore a fresh outfit that looked new. Her hair was wrapped in a bun, and she had an innocent quality that told me she wasn't burned out like some of the others in the customer-service industry. I imagined she was thinking about her flight-attendant training, running through the steps around crash protocol and remembering the importance of keeping a poker face in situations like this one. She must have been told things like, "Stay calm. Passengers react if you react."

But today was different for both of us. In that brief silence we shared a moment of human connection and her eyes seemed to indicate she was looking to *me* for comfort.

She shook her head, "No."

WHAT??? I said to myself. *That's all you got?* She had just confirmed my worst fear. This was it, the big one, as Fred Sanford from the TV show *Sanford and Son* used to bellow while clutching at his heart.

My last minutes on Earth would be spent in aisle twenty-six, flying an airline I didn't even want to be on in the first place.

The turbulence continued. We dropped in altitude, and the airplane shook uncontrollably for several more minutes. The seatbelt was tight around my stomach, which at this point was in knots. I felt that uneasy, near-vomitus feeling like when you're on a roller coaster ride but aren't really sure it's safe. My rate of breathing had shot up, so I decided to try to slow it down. I actually used the exact same breathing technique I taught Sean back in the day. I closed my eyes, sent a message to the higher power and became completely present.

It was clear that the violent turbulence, screaming and general anxiety of the passengers were not going to stop anytime soon. But

I kept at my breathing technique, and after several minutes something amazing happened.

Quietness came over me. Serenity filled my body. The fear of death was replaced by peace. My spirit began to calm me down.

I said a few prayers while continuing to meditate. My breathing slowed even further as my shoulders sank towards the floor like melted chocolate and my hands relaxed. I connected to a place inside and let go of my need to try and change the situation. It was what it was. No amount of thinking and worrying could make it better.

I continued to grow calmer through the violent bursts of turbulence. In the midst of this chaos I experienced a moment of true surrender. I let go of everything that didn't matter. There were no thoughts about my finances, about whether people liked me, whether I was popular, famous, had a nice car or house or my book was a bestseller.

In that quiet space, one thing became abundantly clear: only the special moments in my life mattered. I know it's a cliché, but I literally felt my life flashing before my eyes. All I could focus on were the moments I shared with my children. Several questions flooded my mind:

Did I show them enough that I love them?
Did I make enough time for them?
Will they have an amazing life?
Did I teach them enough?
Did I allow them to teach me enough?
Did I listen with love?

I remembered a time not long before when Kaila, Justice,

Omari and I went roller-skating at the Pier 2 Roller Rink in Brooklyn, overlooking NYC. We had such an amazing time together. It was Omari's and Justice's first time roller-skating. Kaila was finding her groove on the rink after a long time off of it. Watching them laugh, fall, get up, fall and get up again was so cool. It was a great metaphor for life and something I hoped I had helped teach them by example. I never tried to act perfect around my kids. I wanted them to be inspired by seeing how I dealt with my own imperfections. Our day at Pier 2 ended with a stop at the ice cream parlor and an Uber ride home. My kids fell asleep in the car, but when we got home they got a second wind and we watched Netflix together until calling it a night. It had been a day filled with the simple but most important things life has to offer: love, laughter, adversity, a few tears, joy, teachable moments, learning and connection.

Days like these began to pop up in my mind one after another during the turbulence. Memories of walks, games, recitals, talks in the bedroom, holding Kaila as she received stitches from a dog bite, hanging in the city with Justice talking about the birds and the bees, or just laughing and wrestling with Omari in the bedroom— all of these came flooding in. Priceless moments captured in the heart. Nothing was more important in this moment than those memories.

Eventually the turbulence lessened. The worst of it seemed to be over. The flight was still bumpy, but now it felt far from life-threatening. Relief and gratitude rolled through me. The TV screen on the headrest in front of me showed the flight details: there were exactly two hours and twenty-two minutes left in our flight. The flight attendants started serving drinks. When the cart came by, I ordered seltzer water and cranberry, my signature drink. If I drank alcohol, I'd probably have ordered a double shot of anything strong.

The flight attendant I'd connected to earlier was named Brittney. Looking at her without the fear of imminent death in mind, I saw she was a beautiful, statuesque, twenty-something brunette with a nice tan. As she served my drink I learned she was from New Mexico. We laughed together about the moment we'd shared confirming each other's worst fears. She acknowledged that she'd been worried about the outcome and been afraid to admit her own fear. This was why she'd hesitated before answering my question.

I thanked her for my drink and jokingly said, "I wondered if admitting that I was worried made me less of a man in your eyes."

Brittney said without hesitation, "I think it shows you're a real man because of it."

Her answer highlighted something for me. Some men believe they always have to act like they have everything under control. But, as Brittney said before moving up the aisle to continue serving drinks, "It's refreshing to let go of the 'front' and be authentic."

The flight continued to smooth out, and I could relax a little. I even allowed a little humor in, thinking, *If this flight had gone down, maybe my computer would've been found, like a black box, and my book could've been a posthumous memoir*. Thankfully this wasn't the case!

Nothing has ever highlighted my real lack of control like that flight from San Antonio to New York. Nothing. It was both the scariest and clearest moment of my life. There is nothing more life-changing than staring death in the face—that moment when you realize half the things you worry about don't even matter. When I believed that this was my final flight, the only things that seemed to matter were the special moments. The only real question I had for myself was this: had I given enough?

In ancient Eastern philosophy, Samurai legend instructs Samurais to die before battle. The philosophy teaches us that fear keeps us from showing up as powerfully as we can. If a Samurai exhibits any fear before battle, he has already lost. The fear becomes disabling and gives his opponent an insurmountable advantage. Samurais prepare for combat by entering a meditative state and allow themselves to die before battle by letting go of the fear of dying.

On my ill-fated flight there was a moment when everything slowed down. I became quiet and found peace—a peace beyond anything I had ever experienced. It was my understanding at the time that everything was over. No matter how I felt about it, this was my reality. Not once did I think about anything material that I had accumulated or the accolades I had received. It was in that moment that I died before battle. But in that death was a spiritual rebirth, a connection to a power greater than I could have imagined, an alignment with a universe that is LOVE, abundance and prosperity. In that moment I knew that the gift of being a father was the greatest gift in the world. I saw that it was through loving service to my children that I learned to be of loving service to others and the world.

Take a moment and ask yourself this question:

Where has fear prevented me from showing up powerfully as a man, father, colleague or partner in my relationships?

Next ask yourself:

Am I willing to release the attachment to that fear and die before going into battle?

What would this mean? That you no longer wait for the perfect time to give your children and family the love you're capable of giving them. That you shift your priorities away from working late hours "just for now." That you let go of the "victim thinking" that you will only be happy after you accumulate enough money, financial security, houses, cars or better relationships.

Let's be honest: that way of being is not serving you. It is not helping you be all you can be.

Take out a piece of paper right now and answer these questions:

1. What really matters to you? What do you value most in life?

2. Project out twelve months from now and write down the date. What will have happened in your life that made the last year amazing?

3. If you don't achieve the extraordinary life, what will be your reason/s for not doing so?

The coolest thing about my experience during the flight from San Antonio to New York is that I felt good about my answers to questions like these. When it seemed like the end of my life was imminent, it turned out that I was content with the life I had created for myself, my children and my loved ones. Given the time we'd spent together, the special moments we'd shared, the stories and memories that would be told after I was gone, I realized that my life had been enough. I realized that I'd been blessed. I realized that I'd always had exactly what I needed.

If my life ended today, I would be complete. While the accomplishments and accolades I've received for my work throughout the years have been great, they aren't what I'm talking about. I'm complete and fulfilled because of the decision I made a few years back to focus on creating a life around what I value most. Here are a few things I believe will be on my (very large) headstone when the time comes:

1. **Fatherhood:** I was the best father I could be and lovingly led my children. I created the space for them to discover who they are, what they love and who they want to be in the world. All three of my children embody this. I left knowing that they know how much I love them and that they were the greatest gift of my life.

2. **Lessons:** I learned so much on this journey called life. I learned from the great times, but most of all I've learned from the trials and tribulations. Life was my greatest teacher. My next greatest teachers were my children. I'm grateful to have been open to learning more from them than they could ever have learned from me.

3. **Service:** A life of making a difference was so fulfilling. I'm proud of the impact of my early work developing programs for youth and families. My later years as a coach and speaker allowed me to touch and impact so many more lives around the world. I saw families come together, businesses flourish and men and women find meaning and purpose in their lives. I'm grateful for the impact that my clients had on me, and I hope my service was enough for them.

4. **Connection and relationships:** It was an honor to be able to build meaningful relationships with some of the most amazing people in the world. I was inspired by so many wonderful people along this journey and have become better because of it. Hopefully, I impacted their lives in the way they impacted mine.

5. **Love:** At the end of the day my guiding principle was to operate from a state of love. I always strived for loving what is—no matter what it was. My hope is that I loved everyone the best I could. My hope is that the people who have been around me felt my love and connection. My hope is that the people I met along the way, from the moment we connected, didn't feel like we were strangers anymore. Whether they were baristas, custodians, flight attendants, college students, teachers, celebrities or anyone else, I hope that I helped them understand that we are all connected.

That's where I'm coming from. Now let's use the Legacy Zone exercises to see what drives you to be the best you can be.

THE LEGACY ZONE

In my story, I shared what I value and the things that matter most in my life. Now I'm going to ask you to do the same.

ACTIVITY #1: "MY LAST DAY"

Ask yourself the following question each day for the next thirty days:

1. If this were the last day of your life, would you still be doing what you're about to do?

2. If your answer is no, what are you willing to change today?

ACTIVITY #2: "MY OBITUARY"

1. Take out a sheet of paper or open your journal.

2. Write out your obituary as if it were written today. Include everything you wanted to do but didn't. Include the unfulfilled dreams, the unkept promises, and the time that ran out on completion (writing a book, apologizing to a loved one, taking your kids camping, etc.). Be as honest and descriptive as possible.

3. Write a second, ideal obituary as if everything you imagined for yourself and your life was fulfilled and complete. What would be included here? What mattered most? What was your impact? What was your purpose?

4. Create an action plan on how you are going to live out your ideal obituary starting today! Take that twelve-month vision you wrote down earlier in the chapter and break it down into smaller steps. Set weekly, monthly and quarterly milestones for yourself.

ACTIVITY #3: "MY VALUES"

Write out five values you will not compromise along the way. (This is to ensure you stay true to yourself as you move forward.)

I will not compromise _____

I will not compromise _____

I will not compromise _____

I will not compromise _____

I will not compromise _____

REFLECTION

Take some quiet time to reflect on the activities.

1. What are you aware of in completing the exercises?

2. What help do you need in being successful with your plan?

8

THE OVERFLOW

The music is not in the notes, but in the silence between.
~ Wolfgang Amadeus Mozart

A few months prior to publishing this book I was sitting in a hotel restaurant in Nashville, Tennessee, with my publisher, Maurice, and his lovely wife, Ilona. Our window overlooked downtown, and as I glanced outside at the day I could've sworn I heard country music rising up from the streets below.

Maurice and I were discussing the final stages of the book launch. I couldn't hold back my excitement thinking about the impact I wanted to have on fathers around the world. I envisioned empowering them to take ownership of their lives, which would in turn positively impact their children, their work and their communities. The conversation flowed in the direction of how important it is to take care of ourselves so that we can then be of true service to others.

I said, "One of the most important ideas I'd like fathers to grasp is how being of service to others—our families, spouses, and the world—starts with being selfish. It has to be about *you*, until you realize it's not about you."

Maurice smiled and said, "Go on. Tell me more."

"One of the biggest transformations I see in the fathers I work with comes when they start focusing on self-care. When they create space for themselves to build their mental, physical and spiritual muscles. At first it feels selfish to some of them. But it's a necessary step. What happens next is inevitable. They start to look and feel better, and their opinion of themselves changes. A shift occurs. What began as an inside journey starts to overflow into their outside world. They become beacons of love, service and commitment. And everyone benefits: their families, their friends and their communities. Service starts with serving yourself. You can't give others what you haven't first given yourself."

Maurice and Ilona both smiled, and Maurice said, "I love that concept and couldn't agree more." Maurice is an avid reader and historian who loves to share inspiring book excerpts. He added, "Mahatma Gandhi once wrote a letter to one of his followers that stated, 'We must keep ourselves fit for service.'"

Now I was the one smiling and nodding my head. "Exactly!"

The point, of course, is that self-care is a necessary first step towards serving others, especially our children. You'll recall in the previous chapter I told you how I make it a point to listen to the safety announcement at the beginning of each flight. There's a reason for that. I used to be like everyone else, annoyed when they turned off my TV to go over those stupid instructions. But one day as I sat there with the TV off and watched the attendant do her thing, she said something I'd heard a hundred times before—but that day it struck me as if for the first time:

"In case of emergency, oxygen masks will drop down in front of you. Please pull the mask down toward your face and place the mask over your mouth and nose. If you are traveling with a child, please attend to yourself first, then the child."

BOOM! There it was, the best parenting advice (and life advice) someone could ever give. Before you can help someone else, you first have to take care of yourself. I can never hear a reminder like this too many times.

We need to first treat ourselves with the same love and compassion that we want to serve the world with. This is what Gandhi was talking about. This is what being "fit" for service means.

The form your own self-care takes is up to you. For some, self-care means prayer or meditation. For others it's exercise, attending trainings, reading or journaling. For many it's some combination of these. My own experience has shown that the deliberate practice of self-care not only enhances my life, but also the lives of those around me. As a father, this practice has been the number one reason I have such great relationships with my children. It's paradoxical to think that a healthy relationship with our children is based in part on not spending time with them. But it's true. We need to spend time alone with ourselves first.

Several years ago my life was completely different from what it is today. I felt overwhelmed. I felt like I could do so much more with myself, my career, my life, but I had a tendency to blame circumstances "outside of my control" for my lot. I was twenty pounds overweight and had no motivation to get in shape. This was a far cry from my basketball-playing days.

In short, I was caught on the hamster wheel of life, trading my time for money. My days were marathons of running from one place to the next, with me longing for them to end so I could go home and veg out watching TV. I knew a lot of people, so I never had a problem socializing, but even going out seemed like a chore.

I'd show up for my kids' games, preoccupied with work and constantly responding to emails. Happiness and peace came only in glimpses.

Until one day it all came to a crashing halt. I woke up depressed, lonely and in a bad place. I'd had tickets to take Kaila to a basketball game the night before but hadn't made it. This made me think of how six months earlier the same thing had happened when I'd planned on taking Justice to the circus. These things were symptomatic of the larger problem: I was feeling so overwhelmed that I wasn't making time for the most important things in life.

I didn't know how to get out of my downward spiral, but I knew that if I didn't reach out for help things would only get worse. The funny thing is, I'm sure people who knew me had no clue how I was feeling, and if you had asked them they'd probably have told you how happy I seemed.

Everyone loved me, but I didn't love myself. I was too busy trying to please others and not spending enough time on myself. The result? I felt empty, isolated and overwhelmed.

The process of self-care and reinventing myself began as I started thinking about the consequences of continuing to live my life this way. I felt sick at the thought of missing out on the most important moments in my children's lives. In this sense, the thought of fatherhood saved me from myself. It pushed me to create an intentional life, one based on *choices*, rather than a default life where I just let things fall where they might. One of my first steps towards reinvention was admitting that I had a problem—and that *I* was the problem.

The beauty in admitting this was that if I was the problem then

I was also the solution.

I took a look at why I felt so burned out, unmotivated and exhausted at the end of the day, and the reason was immediately clear: I wasn't taking time for myself. I was constantly giving to others at work, at home and in the community. But this life left me tired, frustrated and constantly feeling like I was on a rollercoaster ride, holding on for dear life. I'd experience periods of time when things would be going well, but eventually I'd crash. Have you ever felt the same way?

Next I looked at what was going on inside me and how it compared to life outside me. Inside there was constant noise: noise in my head, noise around the house, noise in the streets and noise at work. Noise. Noise. Noise. Noise. I'd told myself that living amidst chaos kept me sharp and that hustling was the only way to find success. I believed that someday in the undetermined future, after I worked my butt off, I would have time to slow down and enjoy life.

That "someday" way of thinking was my first sign that I was living a "destination addiction."[2] This is when we think that things will be great once we get to a certain place in our relationships, career or life in general. For example, have you ever thought things like the following?

- Once I get enough money I'll be happy.

- Once I get enough money I'll be able to spend more time with my kids.

- Once I get a better job everything will be better.

---

[2] The term "destination addiction" was coined by British psychologist Robert Holden, Ph.D.

- Once I find a mate I'll feel complete.

In my own case, my someday never came. Until I created it.

One of my favorite quotes helped me shift my perspective. Mozart said,

The music is not in the notes, but in the silence between.

If all we had were note after note with no breaks between the individual notes, all we'd end up with would be noise. Just like the noise of dissatisfaction in our heads. Just like the noise of self-doubt. The noise of our thoughts about "someday."

I realized I needed silence in between the noise in my life. I reflected on the rare quiet times I'd had with my children, when everything was peaceful. I remembered story time before bedtime or just chilling out and sitting on the stoop of the house. Those times were perfect, *and* they were away from the noise.

To achieve that level of stillness again I saw that I had to change not only my mindset and entire routine, but also a range of habits and ways of thinking that simply weren't serving me.

THE GREATEST LOVE OF ALL

I used to be the guy who only slept five hours a night, with the cell phone and computer right next to the bed. At the sound of the alarm I would jump out of bed, respond to emails, jump on social media and rush out to try to serve the world. I wore this way of doing things like a badge of honor. The fact that I didn't need much sleep and could wake up and immediately start getting things done seemed not only to make sense but also to be the honorable thing to do.

One day a mentor of mine said to me, "Let me get this

straight. The first thing you do when you wake up is try and serve the world without first taking time to serve yourself?"

His comment hit me like a ton of bricks. I realized in that moment that my morning "routine" wasn't intentional or even that productive. Neither was the rest of my day, for that matter. I was being reactive, running around disheveled and disorganized. I would respond to things on the fly, as they came at me, instead of with thoughtful, intentional practices.

So I decided to spend the first hour of my day practicing self-care. In that hour I would not touch my phone, check emails or get on my computer.

At first it was difficult. I felt like I was wasting time and worried I wouldn't get enough done. I had to force myself to put my cell phone and computer on the other side of the room so I wouldn't automatically reach for them when I woke up. But once I began dedicating the first hour of my day to giving myself the love and attention I needed to be at my best, my life and business took off. I began getting more things done before 10 a.m. than most people complete by the end of the day. I was more present, attentive and creative in my interactions with the world. I genuinely felt more energetic, positive, and open to new possibilities. I became a more attentive parent, less serious and more playful with my children. I enjoyed my family and friends more. It was amazing how this "oxygen mask" really allowed me to breathe life into everything I did.

Our being consists of mental, physical and spiritual parts. By creating a self-care routine that honors each of these, you'll see a dramatic change in how you relate to yourself, your family and the world. You are a special man, father, partner and leader. You count. You matter. If you want to have a life where you achieve more AND find fulfillment in each day, then create the space for self-love.

Cue up Whitney Houston because it's the greatest love of all! More importantly, it's another form of leadership: the ability to love yourself fully so that you can fully love others.

It's something your future self will thank you for.

P.O.W.E.R. HOUR

I've developed a morning routine I call the P.O.W.E.R. Hour. My clients have found it to be a game changer. Use what works for you and leave the rest. What I share are tools, not rules.

P – peace: (10-20 minutes). The first twenty minutes of my day are spent in quiet mediation and prayer. This allows me to slow everything down and give myself time to be present and relaxed.

O – openness: (10 minutes). I take time each morning to journal about gratitude and what would make the day ahead extraordinary. I've found that the only way to find success, happiness and joy in any given day is to first define what those things would mean to me that day.

W – who? what? why?: (5 minutes). These are the three big questions I ask myself in the morning:

Who needs me today? The answer to this question allows me to be more selective about where I'm spending my time and energy. I can't be everything to everyone, and being intentional about my time keeps me from becoming overcommitted. The only people who make this list every day are my children.

What am I about to do today? This question focuses me on the most important tasks to move forward. I keep it between two to three tasks that will be the most fulfilling if I complete them.

Why am I about to do that? Steve Jobs said he asked himself this question daily: "If today were the last day of my life, would I want to do what I'm about to do today?"[3] If the answer was "no" for more than a few consecutive days, he changed what he was doing. Now I ask the same of myself, and this allows me to create my day rather than fall victim to circumstances.

E – exercise: (15-20 minutes). Stretching, moving, running, yoga or calisthenics are all great options. I jump on a rebounder, followed by stretching and calisthenics each morning to get the blood pumping.

R – reading: I read inspiring books, listen to podcasts or watch TED Talks. This practice has helped cultivate a mindset and attitude of abundance (what I do have) rather than scarcity (what I don't).

STOP SAYING "YES"

One of my first mentors, a productivity guru, taught time management techniques and strategies. At first I was amazed at all the shortcuts I learned that I could use to get more out of my day. But eventually I realized that even with more time I still felt unfulfilled. In fact, I still didn't know exactly what a productive day looked like. I realized that my problem wasn't time

---

[3] "Steve Jobs – "If Today Were The Last Day Of My Life...." Chuck Balsamo. Accessed July 10, 2017.
http://chuckbalsamo.com/2011/10/steve-jobs-if-today-were-the-last-day-of-my-life/.

management. It was what I was doing with myself. What, I asked, did having more time really mean to me if I still wasn't doing the things I valued? I was gaining extra time in my day just to become busier doing stuff I didn't want to do. Where's the freedom in that?

I began to see that one of the main problems with managing time is people pleasing. In other words, saying "yes" when you really want to say "no"! If I wanted to create more time in my day for my children, I had to start saying "no" to things that weren't a priority and "yes" to the things that were. So I took a look at the commitments in my life that I needed to say "no" to.

One of the biggest factors in burnout is a constant outward flow of energy without a reciprocal return flow. This is why self-care is one of the first things I look at with fathers when helping them set out on a journey of transformation. Fathers often share with me how much time and energy they spend giving of themselves to their children, spouses and businesses without pausing to refuel. We complain that we're "stretched" and never have enough time for ourselves. We say it's selfish to think of ourselves, often sounding like martyrs.

Stop it already! Taking care of ourselves will impact our children and world far more than giving of ourselves until we're burned out and there's nothing left to give.

LAUGH AND PLAY DAILY

One day take time to sit at a playground and watch how much joy children exude. It's become abundantly clear to me that children are much happier than adults, and the ability to play is one of the big reasons for this. Studies about play and joy have been conclusive around this subject. People who are happier are more productive and fulfilled, and they generally live longer lives. I tell people, "Growing up is a trap—don't do it! Keep a playful spirit!"

Laughing and playing with your children can be a fun form of self-care and help you to not take yourself so seriously. Be silly, get on the floor and act crazy with your kids. Fill your days with joy. I was a little less playful with my older children when they were younger, but over time I realized that they really love being silly too. One day my youngest son Omari wanted to jump into a rain puddle. I smiled, took his hand and jumped in with him. I didn't worry about whether or not his sneakers got ruined. We had fun! He and I also have a blast when we find something funny. Recently it was his newest toy: a fart maker. When he pushes it we both laugh uncontrollably.

My daughter Kaila also has a wonderful sense of humor. Every once in a while I'll suddenly pick her up and spin her around in public, embarrassing her as she fakes like she wants me off. Meanwhile she's laughing and teases, "Dad you play too much!"

Now my son Justice is the one who usually makes the first joke, beating me to the punch. He has a keen sense of humor and often pokes fun at my success. He'll say things like, "Dad, now that you're out here blowing up, I'd like a Lamborghini." We share laughs all the time, and all three of my children have taken that quality with them into their lives outside the family.

Life is meant to be lived, so live it with fun and joy by yourself and with your children. Embrace the spirit of play!

TIME ISN'T MONEY

One of my clients is a big player in the financial industry. One day he shared his favorite quote with me: "We go our entire life trading our time for money, only to get to the end of our life and wish we could trade the money for more time."

BAM, mic drop!

Earlier in my life I found myself doing just that: trading my time for money, sacrificing the very things I said I loved most (children, family, personal goals). The bank account filled up but it never seemed to be enough. I'd bought into the belief that I needed to make big sacrifices to reach that ever-elusive goal of freedom. But when you buy into this belief, you eventually notice (as I did) that the goal line always seems to move further and further away the harder you try to reach it. In my own case, I found I'd get more *things* but never seem to be fulfilled. It was never enough.

Does that sound familiar to you?

If we take time to slow down to the speed of life, miraculous things begin to happen. We start creating a life of fulfillment. We nourish our souls and find fulfillment in the here and now, regardless of what's going on outside us. We discover an inner peace and joy that we can tap into each and every day.

When I talk with clients about self-care, one of the first things they'll usually say is, "I just don't have the time." Think about that for a moment. We don't have time for what? To love and nurture ourselves, eat right and take care of our bodies?

If we don't have the time now, when will we? When will we become a priority in our own lives? After the kids go away to college? When we retire?

We've been bamboozled, hoodwinked and led astray. That day of joy and fulfillment never comes—unless we create it right here, right now.

RULE #1: IT'S NOT ABOUT YOU

It's all about you until you realize it was never about you.

My youngest son Omari inspired me to write this chapter. A few days before my manuscript was due to the publisher, he came into the bathroom as I was about to take a shower. He was wearing his Teenage Mutant Ninja Turtles pajamas, and big crocodile tears streamed down his innocent little face.

"Why are you crying?" I asked, picking him up.

He said, "I'm sad because I was thinking about grandpa's funeral and if you and mommy were going to be gone one day."

Omari's maternal grandfather had passed away a few weeks before. His ability to speak his truth so directly surprised me. I tightened my hug and gave him a kiss. "I love you," I said. "Daddy plans on being here a very long time. I'm trying to have front row tickets to your games and grow old."

Omari gripped me tighter and said, "I love you."

My heart sank, and once again I opened up with love. Isn't this the point though? We're all going to die one day, but it's my obligation to take care of myself, practice healthy habits and make the best decisions so that I can have the greatest impact on my children.

INVEST IN A TEA CUP AND SAUCER

People expect me to be at my best when I arrive at their business, conference or home. They don't care if the flight was delayed or if the lady next to me was snoring the whole time or if I had a short turnaround from my last coaching client or speaking event. They expect me to be on point and ready to help them create new possibilities in their lives and businesses. Similarly, my children and family don't want to hear that I'm too tired to make it to the basketball game or dance recital or dinner. They want to know they have all of me, not just the leftovers or scraps after life has chewed me up and spit me out. They want to know that I can be just as attentive to their needs and that they're a priority. So it's important that I take care of myself so that I can take care of them.

Do this for me: Picture a teacup, filled to the brim, sitting on a saucer. The tea inside the cup represents all we have to offer to our children, family and the world. As fathers, providers, employees, business owners, partners, we are often serving people with our time, energy and money directly from our cup. Without a commitment to self-care, our cup will eventually run dry. At that point we get overwhelmed, overstretched and burned out.

Self-care is the antidote to the empty cup. Self-care is how we can constantly fill our cups to the point where we create an overflow onto the saucer. By constantly creating the overflow, we can shift into serving people *from the saucer*, thus allowing our cups to stay full. The cup never gets empty because people receive the overflow created by our attention to ourselves. We never get empty. Instead we have *more* energy, more space, more time—and ultimately a more fulfilling life.

Once you're able to serve from the saucer you'll realize it's not even about you. That's right: fatherhood isn't about you. Helping people isn't about you. Making a difference isn't about you. Your legacy, impact and influence on the world will not be about what you acquired. It will be about how you contributed.

Fill your cup, create an overflow and discover how abundant

life can be when you serve from a full cup. The time, energy and love you want to give others flows freely when you first give it to yourself.

> "No such thing as spare time,
> No such thing as free time,
> No such thing as down time,
> All you got is life time,
> Go!"
>
> ~ Henry Rollins, "Shine"

THE LEGACY ZONE

Here are a few ways to create space in your life and make yourself the priority. When you integrate these practices into your life you'll see amazing results in performance, mindset, and clarity of purpose.

SELF-CARE ROUTINE

Experiment with the P.O.W.E.R. hour or your own version of it for the next thirty days. Track how you feel along the way in a journal.

CREATING AN INTENTIONAL LIFE

1. A good day starts the night before, and a good week starts the week before. Pick a day (the same one every week) and spend fifteen to twenty minutes reviewing your week. Use this time to recognize your successes as well as things you still need to improve upon.

2. Create a priority list of the things you enjoy doing. Examples might include going to the gym, meditating, spending time with your child, reading, skydiving, playing golf, being outdoors or hanging out with friends.

3. Pull out your calendar and create the week you want for yourself. Block out time in your calendar to ensure that you have standing appointments with yourself to engage with the items on your priority list.

9

THE 36ᵗʰ CHAMBER OF SHAOLIN

> If you light a lamp for someone else,
> it will also brighten your path.
>
> ~ Nichiren Daishonin

As a kid, my favorite day of the week was Saturday. It was the day I felt completely free and without worry. I didn't have to wake up early for school, do homework or prepare for the next day. I could spend all of Saturday morning eating breakfast and watching cartoons if I wanted to.

But the real fun began when the clock struck noon. Then the old Shaw Brothers Martial Arts Movies started up on TV. I wouldn't dare miss a single one. Even if I were outside playing with my friends, we'd run home so as not to miss a second of that week's movie. You might remember them: these were the movies where the mouths of the actors moved, then after a second their words followed in English. The dubbing was such that the mouths never matched the sound. But nothing was lost in translation for us kids.

Kung fu movies were my introduction to eastern philosophy—as expressed by flying guillotines and Shaolin monks with superpowers far superior to those of any Marvel superhero. I thought these guys were amazing. When the shows were over, my friends and I would head outside to practice our kung fu moves on each other. I'd even challenge my opponent like they did in the movies: first by moving my lips soundlessly, then shouting, "Hey you! Want to fight?! Fight me!" I'd follow up with a kick and my best kung fu stance.

Most every kung fu movie I saw contained a life lesson. There was usually a student-teacher relationship that brought these to life. There were lessons about learning, rites of passage, respect, honor, perseverance and choices, to name a few. The greatest students often started by questioning everything, including their teacher. Some students were outright defiant until their teacher calmly brought them back to earth with a Jedi-like mind trick, or tossed them through the air with a simple head-nod.

One of my favorite movies was *The 36ᵗʰ Chamber of Shaolin*. It tells the story of a young boy (who eventually adopts the name San Te) who attempts to sneak into a temple to learn the ancient kung fu techniques. The monks initially reject him as an outsider, but the chief abbot takes mercy on him and lets him stay. San Te is required to do menial work around the monastery for one year before formal training begins (similar to what Daniel must do in *The Karate Kid*).

Each element of San Te's training takes place in a distinct chamber in the temple. The completion of a chamber signifies acquisition of a new discipline of kung fu and brings the student one step closer to mastery. San Te completes the thirty-five chambers of teachings faster than any other student has ever done. He tells the abbot he wants to create a new chamber to help students defend themselves and their families against oppression.

The abbot abruptly banishes him, knowing that the student's work at the temple is done, and that San Te's mission is too big to keep him at the temple. San Te leaves confused but undeterred. He defeats the oppressors of his people and returns to the monastery to create a new chamber: the thirty-sixth. The abbot had realized this day would come and knows his student has surpassed him in many ways. He looks on San Te with pride.

The 36th Chamber of Shaolin reminds me of the relationship between my first-born and myself. When I look into my daughter Kaila's eyes, I see that she's become the student who's left the temple. In her short life she has taught me many lessons about life—starting from the day I found out that I was going to become a father.

I was twenty-three years old and living in a college dorm room when my girlfriend Michelle and I found out we were going to have a child. When Michelle told me she was pregnant, I was overwhelmed with thoughts and emotions. For some reason I felt the need to act like I wasn't freaking out even though I really was. I thought to myself, if Michelle could read my mind right now she'd be running for the hills.

Don't get me wrong: I was excited to welcome a new life into the world, but at age twenty-three I had no idea what being a father meant. I wondered whether I had enough money (with no job lined up), whether I'd still be able to pursue my dreams (although I had no idea what my purpose was) or even if I would still be able to simply hang out with my friends once in a while.

Most of all I asked myself: Am I ready for this?

In the months that followed I had a nervous pit in my stomach. We told our families—and thank goodness for loving parents who stepped up and helped ease some of our anxiety. Our mothers were amazingly supportive, which really helped. We went to prenatal appointments and Lamaze classes and bought encyclopedia-sized books about what to expect when we were expecting. I skimmed through them but couldn't wrap my head around what it all would be like. Really I had no idea what I was doing, even though my ego told me I had to convey an image to the outside world of being cool, calm and collected. So I acted as if I had it all together. I didn't ask anyone other than family members what it was like to be an expectant father. Men I knew at the time weren't talking about their feelings about fatherhood, so at times I felt very alone.

None of that seemed to matter when, in August of that year, Kaila arrived. I told you in the introduction how my world changed when I first held her. A softer side of me emerged. I had been conditioned for years not to show this side of myself. What we call "life" now made sense.

That day was the beginning of a new life for me, the beginning of an extraordinary journey filled with love, compassion, commitment, support, empathy, leadership and a learning that never stops. As a first-time father, I often learned my greatest lessons by making some of my greatest mistakes. My first one may have been finding Kaila's pants soaked with urine because I didn't secure her diaper properly. That was only the beginning. I've made so many fumbles along the way, but I've also come to realize that this was part of the process of growing into being a father. My daughter changed my perspective about everything. Not least I became more aware of how men speak to and treat women because I now had a baby girl.

Throughout the years I have done all I can to teach Kaila

about life, love and the world. She's developed into a wonderful human being: inquisitive, smart, funny, possessing a warm, loving heart and always seeking her own truth. Raising a teenage daughter has been fun and, at times, anxiety-provoking. Fun because our father-daughter bond has flourished through insightful conversations, laughter and life lessons. Anxiety-provoking because like all parents I've had to start letting go of the reigns a bit, letting Kaila stay out later, start driving, and so on. So of course I knew she'd be exposed to drugs, alcohol and sex. (It doesn't help when I remember what I was like as a teenager and think about my daughter dating a guy like me back then. UGH!)

Kaila's also been instrumental in helping teach me a lesson of fatherhood that's taken years to learn, but which is also the greatest of them all: *keep a student's mindset.*

It reminds me of the abbot and the student in *The 36th Chamber of Shaolin.* I've come to realize that our children watch and listen more than we think. Children begin to form their own interpretations of life and evolve in ways that outpace us. My daughter is like the student in *The 36th Chamber of Shaolin,* and I'm like the abbot. Kaila is beginning her life out in the world, and she returns from time to time to show me a thing or two. I know that she will continue to teach me from her own journey. Already I've learned that learning from her is the greatest reward of being her father. And so I keep a student's mindset on each step of my own journey, in fatherhood and in life. I have learned to love being the student.

As fathers we often feel the need to be perfect role models for our children, but this can never be a reality. Perfection doesn't exist, and constantly striving for it leaves us disheartened. Choose progress over perfection and you will find more fulfillment, joy and happiness. We are all flawed individuals with shortcomings that can get in the way of our growth. Besides, our goal as fathers isn't to create "mini-me's"—new-and-improved versions of ourselves. In fact, trying to do this robs our children of the chance to become who they are meant to be—and it also robs us of the gift of fatherhood, of learning and growing as men. In order to receive this gift we have to be open to the lessons our children teach us. Our highest job is to create a space for these spirits to grow into the best versions of themselves.

Maybe some of you are saying to yourselves, "Yeah, right. I don't believe my child can teach me more than I teach them."

I hear you, and I ask that you be open. These realizations didn't come to me overnight. I speak from experience in helping raise a now nineteen-year-young woman through all her stages of development up to the present. I'm also helping raise two other children, ages fifteen and seven, with a new set of eyes that were opened wider and wider while raising Kaila. I also speak from my experience listening to and coaching hundreds of men over the years.

So trust me when I promise that having a student mindset as a father is a game changer. It opens your path of freedom as a father and in life. You no longer have to act like you've got it all together. You're allowed to be human. You're allowed to make mistakes. You're allowed to be vulnerable. And when you give yourself permission to just be yourself, your relationships and your life are enhanced.

Here are some of the most important life lessons I've learned from my own personal guru, my daughter Kaila.

LOVE AND GRATITUDE

In 2013, I was invited to give the keynote at the Real Dads Network Annual Awards Ceremony in Brooklyn. I was honored to be asked, and I wanted to share the moment with my first child and only daughter, so I extended Kaila an invitation to join me. She was sixteen at the time. She accepted, and I couldn't have been happier. The event was several months away, so I gave her the link to the website so she could learn about what I was supporting.

***

The day of the ceremony arrives. Summer is underway. All the schools are winding down and people are spending more time outside. The buzz in New York City is vibrant and energizing. I've prepared a forty-five-minute keynote speech and read it over one more time before heading out. It weaves together personal stories and thoughts on fatherhood, leadership and transformation. If I've done my job right, the speech will send fathers a message of hope.

Kaila and I take the 2 train into Brooklyn. She looks beautiful in her "superstar celebrity" sunglasses and cool Forever 21 threads. I'm so happy to have her by my side. We arrive, and it's immediately clear the event is something magical. Smiles and laughs light up the room. Kaila and I have a lot of fun together. I enjoy seeing the pride the men there feel in being fathers. I'm inspired and feeling right at home.

There are some wonderful speakers and a musical performance by a super-talented youth group. Then comes the ceremony, during which the "Real Dad of the Year" awards are announced. The award recognizes a few fathers as being extraordinary presences in the lives of their children and communities. To win the award, a father needs to be nominated by the Real Dads Network organization. After the father is nominated, their children are called directly, asked to write a piece about how special their father is—and are sworn to secrecy. I'm looking forward to this part of the event, excited for whoever is nominated and eager to hear about their impact directly from their children.

Kaila and I sit near the stage, listening to the MC, Derek Phillips, read the nominations. The accompanying stories are heartfelt and inspiring, and I'm moved by each nomination. They make me proud to be a father myself.

Derek adjusts the microphone and starts to read the last nomination:

My father is one of the most influential people in my life. He is supportive of everything I choose to do in life and continues to help me become a better person as I grow and flourish into adulthood. There have been countless times in which my father has picked me up from low points in my life I thought I could never recover from, but he has been there to help guide me into making the right decisions and pushing through the rough times. My father showed me what love and respect from a man should look like and how a real man should treat a woman. He has showed me that I should always know my worth and never lower myself in order to please others. Throughout my life he has been an amazing role model and has shown me what love is. Unlike others, my dad wasn't my first heartbreak, but he was one who showed me unconditional love. My dad sticks by my side, and even when times get tough or we have disagreements, I know I can always call on my dad to be there to help pick up the pieces.

From feeding the homeless on Thanksgiving to wrapping Christmas presents for underprivileged kids, my father has shown me the importance of kindness and selflessness, and he continues to do so every day. Not a day goes by that I don't thank my father for the life lessons he has taught me and remind him how grateful I am for his presence and everything he has provided for me. My dad is my hero and I love him more than anything in this world.

As Derek reads this beautifully written piece from a daughter to her father, my eyes begin to water. At the end, he looks up and says, "This Real Dad of the Year award goes to Devon Bandison."

I don't know what to do with myself. I'm touched beyond words—and completely surprised by the nomination. I had no idea that Kaila had taken the time to do this for me. Everything is perfect. Kaila's words warm my heart and calm my spirit. I feel a sense of unconditional love. Humbled, I walk onto the stage with Kaila to accept the award and take pictures. I am moved to tears by the joy that reverberates through my spirit.

I'm speechless, but I still have to do my job as keynote speaker!

***

I hope all fathers can experience what it feels like to know that you have made a lasting impact on your child's life. In all honesty, I cared far less about the award that night and much more about hearing my daughter's heart speak. I have received many awards and accolades over the years, but this was by far the best. There isn't even a distant second. In that moment, Kaila once again became the teacher and I the student. She showed me how gratitude speaks from the heart. She showed me what's really important in life: love, gratitude, support, and service, to name a few. She put meaning to those words and forever deepened my understanding of them.

Kaila's words may have echoed lessons she's learned from me, yet what I have realized is that she's taught me more than I could ever teach her. In fact, she's been one of my greatest teachers.

LISTENING, INTERNALIZING AND SELF-WORTH

One day Kaila called me from Florida.

"Hey Dad, what's up? I was nominated for homecoming queen and it's coming up soon."

I responded with the pride and joy of a father. "I'm so happy for you, Queen! You're beautiful inside and outside. Duh, of course you were nominated!"

I immediately cleared my calendar and booked my plane ticket to Florida. This was a time I had to show up for my daughter.

As a senior in high school, Kaila's nomination for homecoming queen was a BIG deal. Michelle and Kaila had done all the necessary pre-homecoming preparation. They'd spent countless hours finding the right dress and doing hair, makeup and everything else that young women want done before an event like this.

On the day of the football game, I had the honor of escorting my daughter out to midfield with the rest of the nominees. As we walked, Kaila squeezed my arm tight and I could feel her tension.

I said, "Are you nervous?"

Her response floored me. "I'm a little nervous, Dad, but

whether I win or lose, you've taught me that I'm already a queen. I don't need other people's validation to confirm that."

She was right. Throughout her childhood I would point out certain things she did, like working hard, treating people with kindness and being giving of herself to others. I'd explain that it is her character that makes her a true queen. On the day of homecoming I'd been caught up in "Dad brain," thinking that it'd be a crushing blow to my child's self-esteem if these people didn't make the right choice! She slowed me down and brought me back to the moment. She had already developed self-worth along the way to growing up. She had already "got" that she was more prepared than me to stand up in the middle of that football field, regardless of the outcome.

And in case you're wondering: Kaila wasn't crowned homecoming queen that night. She handled herself with style, dignity and grace, and she shone brighter than any star in the sky. I couldn't have been more proud of her. (And, of course, she was and always will be my Queen.)

STANDING UP FOR YOUR VISION

In August 2015, Michelle and I brought Kaila to college to settle in for her freshman year. As we entered the dorm room, I had flashbacks to my own college years. Kaila would be sharing a suite with several other girls. There were three bedrooms, each with two beds, and they would all share a bathroom. I had a similar set up (with guys, of course!) during my student days at Belmont Abbey.

Seeing her room made me feel a bit nostalgic. I recalled the innocence, awkwardness and sense of the unknown that I'd felt being sent to live on my own for the first time. I also reflected on all the amazing experiences I've had since then. I found myself fighting back tears as I thought, *My little girl is all grown up and ready to live on her own, and I am proud of the woman she has become. I can still remember the first time I held her in my arms in the delivery room and how precious she was with her big cheeks. Now she's a young woman standing on her own two feet.*

Kaila has been such a gift in my life. I'm so grateful for her. I know that I haven't always agreed with her decisions. Sometimes I was right, sometimes she was, and sometimes we both were. When she believed in something, she stood up for it. For example, Michelle and I thought that Kaila was nonchalant about college, but she wasn't. She took care of her business and proved us wrong. She made her own list of the schools that interested her and was unsure for some time which way she wanted to go. All on her own she researched material on campus life, activities, dorm rooms, majors and what each college offered. I was so proud of her for setting up her vision.

As Michelle and I were about to leave, I turned to Kaila and said, "Thank you for showing me once again how special of a woman you are," and gave her a giant hug and kiss. She had picked the perfect college for herself, and it had been a decision only she could make. Her path was well thought out and inspiring.

I could see it was time for the abbot to lovingly banish her from the temple so she could journey out on her own.

GIVING PEOPLE THE ABILITY TO MAKE THEIR OWN CHOICES

In another chapter I mentioned that my daughter did not speak to me for about a month. This was another lesson for me. In this particular case, even though I had the best intentions I totally missed the mark.

Kaila wanted to buy a car. She told her mother and me that she'd save up some of her own money and asked if we could help her with the rest, as long as she could pick out the car she liked. We agreed.

Not long after I learned my sister was buying a new car and had decided to give the old one to my mom and stepdad, Roy. They in turn generously told me they'd like to gift Kaila my sister's old car. They put a lot of effort into getting the car serviced and ready for the big surprise. (My mom is the best and Roy has been a great guy in our lives.)

I thought to myself, *I can't miss this opportunity to save some money and present Kaila with her first car! And while the Dodge Charger is a hooptie,[4] I'll be killing two birds with one stone! Every child should start with an old car so they can learn to appreciate it. That's how I started out so this must be true. This is a brilliant plan!*

I ran the idea by Kaila's mother, Michelle. She was hesitant, uneasy, and she asked, "Don't you think we should give Kaila a heads up?"

"NO!" I said, still excited. "This'll be a great surprise and a wonderful moment!"

When the time came, Kaila and I drove from her college in Boca Raton to Michelle's house in Orlando. Sitting out front was the Dodge Charger with a big red bow on top. Kaila smiled, thanked everyone and seemed to genuinely appreciate receiving her first car.

But I sensed something more behind her words, and when we

---

[4] A beater.

had a minute alone I asked her, "What's up?"

"Dad," she said. "I would've liked to have been given a heads-up. I wanted the option to save money for another car."

I immediately got defensive. In my mind I called her ungrateful and wrong. Thankfully, I kept it to myself, standing silently and not responding (though my face probably said it all).

But she wasn't wrong, and neither was I. She was just expressing how she felt. She was upset with me in the moment, and when she returned to school she didn't want to talk to me for a while.

When we finally spoke, she said, "Dad, it wasn't about the car. It was about allowing me to make my own choices in life."

The lesson was clear: stop acting like I always know what's best for my daughter. Sometimes as fathers we ought to slow down and listen to make sure we really hear our children. If I had listened, I would have heard loud and clear what mattered most to her around the car. She wasn't being ungrateful, but it was important to her that she have the chance to make the choice herself. My daughter taught me a great lesson about listening without my own agenda in the way. Thank you, Guru!

(As a footnote, she really *was* grateful for the car. She grew into it and now plans to trade it in next year for an upgrade.)

***

When the student returned, the abbot had already heard about his exploits in the world, teaching students and reclaiming the village from the oppressors. Strangely enough, it was the abbot who had learned the greatest lesson of all. He took pride in knowing that he had done his job in preparing the young student for life, and that in letting go he was allowing the student to become his own master. And so great things happened for the student, for himself and for the world. The student became master and the master returned to his truest state, that of student.

You have no doubt heard the saying, "When the student is ready, the teacher appears." With each passing day that I ready myself with a student mindset, it's become clear that my children are the greatest teachers of all.

THE LEGACY ZONE

LOVE, GRATITUDE, PLAY AND CREATIVITY

Take this ninety-day challenge to create more gratitude, love and creativity in your life.

1. Each day write down three things you're grateful for and three things you love about your child.

2. Every day communicate to your child the three things you love about them.

3. During this ninety-day period, build in fifteen-minute blocks each day to connect with your child with no rules (for example, to talk, wrestle, laugh, draw or build something).

4. At the end of the ninety days, have a conversation with your child. Ask them what they've learned from you and what you've learned from them.

5. Co-create a learning experience with your child (for example, build a tree house, learn a language, watch a new sport, read a new book).

LEARNING

1. Make a list of things that interest you and which you would like to learn more about.

2. Research books, classes and seminars on one skill you'd like to learn or improve upon.

3. Commit to learning a new skill for ninety days and follow through on doing it.

4. Share what you're learning and have learned with your family and friends.

5. Teach someone else the skill you've learned.

10

LIVE YOUR LEGACY

Legacy is not what's left tomorrow when you're gone. It's what you give, create, impact and contribute today while you're here that then happens to live on.

~ Rasheed Ogunlaru

I'd like to tell you a story about Michelangelo and the marble statue of David.

For the fathers with little ones, I'm not talking about the Teenage Mutant Ninja Turtle named Michelangelo. No, I'm referring to the famous Italian artist. Legend has it that one day a priest was so inspired by seeing the beauty of Michelangelo's marble statue of David that he was moved to tears. He set out on a mission to thank the artist for bringing such beauty into the world.

When the priest finally found Michelangelo, he fell at the artist's feet and said, from the bottom of his heart, "Michelangelo, thank you for creating such a wonderful piece in the statue of David."

Michelangelo said, "Thank you. But I didn't create the statue of David."

The priest looked confused.

Michelangelo continued, "The beauty of David was always in

the marble. My only job was to chip away what *wasn't* David."

Michelangelo, I couldn't have said it better. Thank you.

Fathers, do you see it? You guys are already great. Everything you want, whether it's abundance, connection, love, forgiveness, leadership, better health, a life that matters, fulfillment and happiness—it's already inside you. My hope is that you use this book as a guide that helps you chisel and chip away at the things that are holding you back.

It's not just fatherhood that we're talking about transforming here. It's your whole life. I've worked with some of the greatest athletes, CEOs and businessmen around the world. The same high performance skills I've taught them translate directly into fatherhood, and vice versa. There are no better peak performers in my mind than fathers who are playing all out. This is who we can be. In fact, it's *who we already are*. David in the marble. We just have to tap into it.

Through the stories and lessons shared in this book, I wanted to show you guys that fatherhood is the gateway to freedom. Financial freedom and freedom from guilt. It opens the door to peace of mind, abundance, joy, fulfillment and happiness. Our personal and professional development no longer have to be separate. They aren't competing priorities but the gifts and opportunities that fatherhood offers to you.

You can have it all.

Yes, you read that right: you can have it all. You can have the wonderful family life, whether you're married or a single father. You can develop the leadership skills that will help you be successful in your career. You can have the financial freedom you once dreamed of. You can have the time to do the things you love the most and the mindset to create it all. You just need to realize one thing:

THERE IS NOTHING WRONG WITH YOU!!!

Nothing. At all. Point blank. Period.

No matter what self-judgment you or anyone else has imposed on you, there is nothing wrong with you. You are a gift to your children, your family and the world. Everything you ever wanted to be or have is inside you. You can't be any less great than the greatness that already lives within you. No book, no program and no amount of money or success can change that.

What I want you to realize is that it's not about simple change—it's about transformation. This transformation is about taking what's already living inside you and sharing it with the world. The love, happiness, joy, fulfillment, financial freedom and success you seek are within you.

Make a commitment right now to stop beating yourself up for not being where you think you should be. I'm serious. You need to STOP IT! You are exactly where you're supposed to be given the tools you've been using thus far.

You now have a new set of tools, a new mindset, and the possibility of creating a new world for yourself and your loved ones. It's time to put your EMOTION into doing so—or rather, it's time to put your energy in to motion. What you invest your energy in creates your reality. If you don't believe me, sit around with a friend who complains about everything and everyone and see how long it takes before you find yourself becoming cynical. A simple shift towards the life you want—towards GROWTH—will create a new world for you. And one of the biggest spiritual principles I have learned is this: if you don't grow, you die.

This is the game of life, and you guys are game changers. But you have to be on the court to be in the game. You can't be a spectator. The magic only happens when you tie up your laces and give it all you have.

Remember I told you about a client of mine, a professional basketball player in the U.S and overseas, who always used to say, "If I miss ten shots in a row, I know that the eleventh is going in"? That's the champion mindset we need as fathers and leaders in the world. Things won't always go our way, so fail forward, learn from the opportunity and then use it as fuel to be even better.

YOUR STARTING FIVE

Jim Rohn once said that you'll be the average of the five people you spend the most time with. And any high performer in business, sports or life needs a team to support their efforts.

So let me ask you: *Who are your starting five?*

If you're a married man and your starting five consists of single guys who hang out late on the weekends, that may not work out so well for you.

If you have a goal of creating a million-dollar business but your starting five averages $50,000 a year, that setup probably won't help you meet your goal.

If you're a father who wants to create a life where you do the things you love while still being an active parent, but you surround yourself with people who always feel overwhelmed, I encourage you to take a second look at the company you're keeping.

Some of the key drivers for success in this world are the people in your circle and community. As fathers, you have many resources at your disposal, many of which you may not even be aware of. Help is out there! I've had the pleasure of serving, learning and working with many supportive organizations. Here are a few:

> *City Dads Group*
> *Real Dads Network*
> *Wharton Work-Life Integration and Total Leadership Program*
> *Good Dad Project*

And at the end of the book you'll find ways to connect and work with me directly as well.

This may be the last chapter of this book, but it's only the beginning for us fathers. We have a chance to make a huge contribution to the world, to lead intentionally created lives. We have the chance to create a living legacy that exists in the present, not at some future time long after we've left the Earth. We can create our legacy while we're still alive. We can be the best fathers, men, sons, partners, and leaders possible. If our work lives on after we're gone, so be it—but that shouldn't be our focus. Let's create a legacy that impacts our children, work and the world right here, right now.

Keep the following in mind. These two factors will keep you on purpose throughout your journey, and they're what all humans strive for:

Growth: I emphasized growth through my stories in this book, and its importance is huge. If flowers don't grow they die. If you aren't consistently pushing past your comfort zone, you will become stagnant. I encourage you to join groups, read books or hire a coach. Your commitment to your growth is your guarantee to your ongoing success.

Contribution: Understanding this principle will single-handedly transform your life. Once we have created our internal happiness, we realize it's not even about us. We learn this as fathers as soon as our children are born, and now we have an opportunity to make an even greater impact using this understanding in the world.

The possibilities are endless.

Fathers, Leaders & Men,

Remember: You are game changers! The best version of yourself and your leadership is based on influence, intimacy and impact. Take what you've learned and share it as it was freely shared with you. Share your stories, your hardships and, most of all, your successes. Other fathers want to hear about you and your leadership. You are needed in this world. You have the capacity to truly influence lives, and it's a great responsibility— one I know you honor. So go out there, play with your children, laugh, joke and create a beautiful life for yourself and those around you.

Live Your Legacy!

Love,

Devon

ACKNOWLEDGMENTS

It's been said it takes a village to raise a child, and that has truly been the case in the creation of this book: a village of amazing human beings who, over the years, have had a profound impact on my life. There are way too many people to mention here. Just know that this journey began long before the writing of this book, and I am humbled and honored beyond measure to have been touched by so many wonderful teachers.

For their work on this book

Maurice "Mo Dawg" Bassett, my publisher, for seeing the vision for this book and understanding that this is a lifelong mission of change. Your guidance and expertise have been invaluable.

Kristi Palma, my "book birth doula," for believing in my ability to develop a transcendent story. Your commitment, love, compassion and guidance as a coach/editor throughout this process unlocked the key to allow for the birth of something special. You are an angel.

Chris Nelson, my editor, for understanding the importance of keeping my voice and the integrity of the work. You're a true professional and a pleasure to work with.

Carrie Brito, my cover artist, for your wonderful creativity and for bringing the essence of this work forward.

Albie Mitchell (front cover) and Mindy Veissid (back cover), for your amazing photography.

Mentors, Friends, Fellow Travelers

James "Goody" Goodwine. Goody, you've been a second

father to me and words will never be able to capture the immense gratitude I have for you. You've been a spiritual guide, teacher and vision of hope. It is such a blessing to enjoy the fruits of our labor, which always come in the right season. I pray that I can one day impact someone's life as profoundly and lovingly as you have mine.

Steve Chandler, my coach, mentor and friend. Steve, you have taught me what being of service to the world looks like through your undying commitment to prosperity, growth and success. You are a model of what integrity and living as your word look like. Your knowledge of sports and hip hop just add another element to your perpetual coolness. Thank you for bringing love and fun to my world and for showing me what prosperity in all aspects of life looks like.

Jason Womack, mentor and friend. If it wasn't for that invite to Ojai (which I called O-Jay) a few years back, I may not have been living my dream today as a coach, speaker and author. Your guidance and support is appreciated more than you could ever know.

Dr. Neil Pessin, mentor and friend. Thank you for taking a shot on me sixteen years ago and for your belief that, "It's what you do from here." Your guidance and support of my dream have helped me become the leader I am today. "Character is destiny."

Thabiti Boone, Matt Schneider and Lance Somerfeld (City Dads Group), Stew Friedman (Wharton), Derek Phillips (Real Dads Network), Larry Hagner (The Good Dad Project), Larry Edwards (Edwards Mentoring Group), Trevor Mulligan (LA City Dads Group), Mychal Sledge (The Sledge Group). All of you are doing amazing work with fathers around the world.

Mike Williams (You SML), Jason "JG" Goldberg (my "built for this" brother), Helen Applebee (we're doing it mate), Chris Dorris (my cool Philly guy/brother), Shandue McNeil (next NBA coach), Dan Lloyd, (good friend/IT genius/password protector), Gayle Bu (greatest assistant in the world), Tony Ubertaccio (the book, *The Prosperous Coach*), Donny Brady (my guy for life/Cayuga Ave) Stella "Nanny 911" Reid (grateful for you/keep building that empire), Michael Ralby (compassionate leader), Dr. Sonali Lal (awesomeness with or without a fest).

Jason Carabello, Jane Evans, Jodi Womack, Melvin Moore, Christina Berkley, Talib "Big Brother Almighty," Bey, Jessica Fear, Kerri Hicks, Foluso Otuyelu, Laura Greenberg, Rich Litvin, Aisha Dean, CD and family. Bellmore Family, the Toogoods, Merlann Pena, Silkia Parilla, 40 Banditz, Elsa Suazo, Debra Thomas, Giovanna Capozza, Paula Elmi, Christine Garcia, Michael McDonald, Lisa Giruzzi, Tanja Bogataj, Johnnie Simmons, Laura Borland, Jeremiah Hopes, Kathy Chandler.

Omar Sharif, I love you, man. Your spirit lives on. The Sharif family, you are always in my heart and spirit. My commitment to be of service and contribute to this world exists in part because I keep your son's spirit and memory with me every day.

All the people I've had the honor of coaching over the years. Thank you for allowing me to be a part of your life and for letting us create miracles together. To my Game Changer Mastermind Group, my apprentices and everyone who has attended one of my workshops, thank you. You all inspire me!

Family

Roy "keep your eye on the prize" Levin, Ashley, Bobby and Robert Jr. Potter. Love you guys. Eve and Joe Sanabria, Todd, Troy and Derek "Iron Man" Peterson, Jimmy Boyce, Hans Bandison, Gerrit Bandison, Melody Marrow, and family.

The Goodwine Family, Vicki Levin, Erick Berkowitz, Iris and Gary Kassoff. Ms. Phyllis Watson, Ms. Mae Smalls, and Ms. Sylvia "Ema" Jelks.

Sending love and light to my grandmas Oma and Nana. I love you both and remember our days with a big smile.

Dorothy Levin, my wonderful mother, hero and biggest supporter. I love you. Words cannot describe how blessed I am to be your son. You sacrificed so much for me to have a better life, and you always believed in me. You taught me what integrity, hard work, commitment and unconditional love are. You paid for sports camps, teams and trips when money was tight because you wanted me to have a good life. You are a gift to the world and a big part of why I can now share my own gifts with the world. Thank you, Mom. You are my hero.

Ludwig Bandison, my father. I am grateful for all the life lessons you've taught me along the way. It took me years to realize that the basketball stories you shared on our train rides were actually life lessons that have guided me throughout my life. Thank you for allowing me to honestly share our entire story, for our relationship and for being a wonderful grandfather. I love you.

My Children's Mothers

I'd like to offer a special thanks to the mothers of my children. When I think of our relationships, I'm filled with gratitude. I'm grateful for their grace, love and commitment to co-parenting our beautiful children. They are amazing blessings in my life and in our children's lives. It hasn't always been easy or smooth sailing by any means, but today we share the most wonderful relationships and have learned to co-parent, respect new people in our lives and show our children what it means to love unconditionally. We are family, and I am a better man because of our experiences together on this journey.

Michelle Morgan, thank you for being such an amazing mother and best friend, and for your love and commitment. It's been an honor to share the last twenty years with you.

Latonia Smalls, thank you for all of your sacrifices and commitment to being a great mother. I appreciate all you've done along this journey and value our friendship.

Simone Jelks-Bandison, thank you for your love and commitment to being a great mother. We've come a long way and I'm grateful for that. I hope to make as much of a positive impact in your life as you have in mine.

My Three Greatest Teachers

Kaila Bandison, my beautiful, smart and amazing daughter. It's LIT fam! Twenty-three years ago you came into my world and changed my life. I couldn't be prouder of the young woman you are today. Every time we speak you open up my heart and mind to something new. It has been such a joy to watch you grow into a woman these past years. There is no limit to what you can achieve. Your humor and love are gifts to me and to the world. I love you so much.

Justice Bandison, my handsome, talented and wonderful son. I admire your intuition and ability to question things, as well as the time we spend talking about life. You're an amazing son and big brother, and you are on your way to do great things in life. Thank you for your loving spirit and support. You always "humbly brag" about what your dad's up to, and I want you to know I'm proud of you and the man you're becoming. I love you so much, and MJ is still the GOAT.

Omari Bandison, my shining light and miraculous son who lights up every room he enters. By the time you read this book we will have enjoyed a few more years of pizza nights, school days, train rides and laughter. Your birth into this world wasn't the easiest, and because of your perseverance I have a whole new perspective on love. You are a special gift and I feel so blessed every time I see your face. Daddy loves you so much!

Love,
Devon

ABOUT THE AUTHOR

Devon Bandison is one of the most sought after success coaches in the world. He works with Fortune 100 Companies and people from all walks of life, including professional athletes and teams, CEO's, salespeople, small-business owners, the top business and life coaches in the world and parents.

Devon was born and raised in New York City and shares the same energetic heartbeat, big personality and commitment to excellence as his hometown. Growing up, his love and hard work in sports resulted in his receiving a basketball scholarship to Belmont Abbey in North Carolina.

After graduation he spent years working in the trenches for a non-profit organization, developing programs for youth, families and first-time fathers in some of the toughest neighborhoods throughout NYC. As Director of this organization he supervised social workers, psychiatrists and managers helping to improve the lives of children and families. He also served on various city and state committees to improve service delivery throughout NYC.

Devon holds a Bachelor of Arts in Psychology and a Master of Arts in Public Administration and is now CEO of the Devon Bandison Company, a global coaching company that specializes in high performance and transformation. He provides leadership development, training and coaching to professionals who want to achieve more in life, at home, at work and in the world.

Devon is an international and TEDx speaker and fatherhood thought leader whose work has been featured in the *Wall Street*

Journal, Huffington Post, Inc. Magazine and *Success Magazine*. He is the creator and leader of the Game Changer Mastermind Group and of various workshops for leaders who are ready to play all-out in life and business.

Devon is the proud father of three wonderful human beings who teach him way more about life and love then he could ever teach them. You can catch him with his children at Friday Night Pizza Nights, Basketball for Breakfast, rap concerts or somewhere else having fun together.

Connect with Devon at www.devonbandison.com.

It's time to
LIVE YOUR LEGACY

You're creating your legacy every day, whether you're a CEO trying to design an intentional culture of leadership in your company or a father striving for the life you've always wanted for yourself and your family. If you're ready to make your vision a reality *now*, here are some ways we can make that happen together.

To learn more about incorporating the principles of *Fatherhood Is Leadership* into your organization, to book me at your next conference or company event through keynotes, seminars, training and coaching opportunities, or to ask about my 1:1 coaching, mastermind groups and workshops, please email:

devon@devonbandison.com

and visit

www.FatherhoodIsLeadership.com

Additionally, if you're a father ready to take the next step in creating the influence, intimacy, impact and income that you want in your life, I invite you to join the *Fatherhood Is Leadership Academy*.

This interactive community of fathers offers access to powerful self-leadership tools and resources to help you find success in your life, relationships, wealth and health, all while creating your own living legacy. Head over to FatherhoodIsLeadership.com/academy to see what's included with your membership (it's a boatload).

Men are most successful and thrive in tribes. When you join the Fatherhood Is Leadership Academy, you'll connect with me and an inner circle of like-minded fathers who will support the transformation of your leadership and life.

Live Your Legacy!

Publisher's Catalogue

Devon Bandison

Fatherhood Is Leadership: Your Playbook for Success, Self-Leadership, and a Richer Life

Sir Fairfax L. Cartwright

The Mystic Rose from the Garden of the King

Steve Chandler

37 Ways to BOOST Your Coaching Practice: PLUS: the 17 Lies That Hold Coaches Back and the Truth That Sets Them Free

50 Ways to Create Great Relationships

Business Coaching (Steve Chandler and Sam Beckford)

Crazy Good: A Book of CHOICES

Death Wish: The Path through Addiction to a Glorious Life

Fearless: Creating the Courage to Change the Things You Can

RIGHT NOW: Mastering the Beauty of the Present Moment

The Prosperous Coach: Increase Income and Impact for You and Your Clients (Steve Chandler and Rich Litvin)

Time Warrior: How to defeat procrastination, people-pleasing, self-doubt, over-commitment, broken promises and chaos

Wealth Warrior: The Personal Prosperity Revolution

Kazimierz Dabrowski

Positive Disintegration

Charles Dickens

A Christmas Carol: A Special Full-Color, Fully-Illustrated Edition

Anthony Drago

Go Prove Something! A Basketball Player's Guide to Legally Using PEDs

James F. Gesualdi

Excellence Beyond Compliance: Enhancing Animal Welfare Through the Constructive Use of the Animal Welfare Act

Janice Goldman

Let's Talk About Money: The Girlfriends' Guide to Protecting Her ASSets

Christy Harden

Guided by Your Own Stars: Connect with the Inner Voice and Discover Your Dreams

David Lindsay

A Blade for Sale: The Adventures of Monsieur de Mailly

Abraham H. Maslow

The Psychology of Science: A Reconnaissance

Being Abraham Maslow (DVD)

Maslow and Self-Actualization (DVD)

Albert Schweitzer

Reverence for Life: The Words of Albert Schweitzer

Margery Williams

The Velveteen Rabbit: or How Toys Become Real

Colin Wilson

New Pathways in Psychology: Maslow and the Post-Freudian Revolution

Join our Mailing List:

www.MauriceBassett.com

MAURICE BASSETT

books for athletes of the mind